Cambridge
BEC Preliminary
4

WITH ANSWERS

Examination papers from University of Cambridge ESOL Examinations: English for Speakers of Other Languages

CAMBRIDGE
UNIVERSITY PRESS

CAMBRIDGE UNIVERSITY PRESS
Cambridge, New York, Melbourne, Madrid, Cape Town, Singapore, São Paulo, Delhi

Cambridge University Press
The Edinburgh Building, Cambridge CB2 8RU, UK

www.cambridge.org
Information on this title: www.cambridge.org/9780521739238

© Cambridge University Press 2009

This publication is in copyright. Subject to statutory exception
and to the provisions of relevant collective licensing agreements,
no reproduction of any part may take place without the written
permission of Cambridge University Press.

First published 2009

Printed in the United Kingdom at the University Press, Cambridge

A catalogue record for this publication is available from the British Library

ISBN 978 0 521 73923 8 Student's Book with answers
ISBN 978 0 521 73924 5 Audio CD
ISBN 978 0 521 73925 2 Self-study Pack

Cambridge University Press has no responsibility for the persistence or accuracy of urls
for external or third-party internet websites referred to in this publication, and does not
guarantee that any content on such websites is, or will remain, accurate or appropriate.
Information regarding prices, train times and other factual information given in this work
are correct at the time of going to print but Cambridge University Press does not
guarantee the accuracy of such information thereafter.

Contents

Thanks and acknowledgements   4

Introduction   5

Test 1   Reading and Writing   20
Listening   36
Speaking   43

Test 2   Reading and Writing   46
Listening   62
Speaking   69

Test 3   Reading and Writing   72
Listening   88
Speaking   95

Test 4   Reading and Writing   98
Listening   114
Speaking   121

Key (including tapescripts and sample answers)
Test 1   124
Test 2   129
Test 3   134
Test 4   139

Speaking test interlocutor frames   145

Sample Answer Sheets   146

Thanks and acknowledgements

The authors and publishers acknowledge the following sources of copyright material and are grateful for the permissions granted. While every effort has been made, it has not always been possible to identify the sources of all the material used, or to trace all copyright holders. If any omissions are brought to our notice, we will be happy to include the appropriate acknowledgements on reprinting.

Unilever PLC for the adapted text on p. 30 'Global challenges, local actions' from the Unilever website www.unilever.com. Reproduced by permission of Unilever PLC; BBC.co.uk for the adapted text on p. 80 'What makes a good boss better?' from www.bbc.co.uk/business/features/bosses/goodboss.shtml; DWP Public Relations for the adapted text on p. 104 'Reducing a supermarket chain's costs' from *MCA Awards 2003*. Reproduced by permission of DWP Public Relations on behalf of Management Consultancies Association (MCA).

Introduction

TO THE STUDENT

This book is for candidates preparing for the Cambridge Business English Certificate Preliminary examination. It contains four complete tests based on past papers.

The BEC Suite

The Business English Certificates (BEC) are certificated examinations which can be taken on various dates throughout the year at approved Cambridge BEC centres. They are aimed primarily at individual learners who wish to obtain a business-related English language qualification, and provide an ideal focus for courses in Business English. Set in a business context, BEC tests English language, not business knowledge. BEC is available at three levels – Preliminary, Vantage and Higher.

The BEC Suite is linked to the five ALTE/Cambridge levels for language assessment, and to the Council of Europe's Framework for Modern Languages. It is also aligned with the UK Qualifications and Curriculum Authority's National Standards for Literacy, within the National Qualifications Framework (NQF).

BEC	Equivalent Main Suite Exam	Council of Europe Framework Level	UK NQF Level
	Certificate of Proficiency in English (CPE)	C2 (ALTE Level 5)	
BEC Higher	Certificate in Advanced English (CAE)	C1 (ALTE Level 4)	Level 2*
BEC Vantage	First Certificate in English (FCE)	B2 (ALTE Level 3)	Level 1
BEC Preliminary	Preliminary English Test (PET)	B1 (ALTE Level 2)	Entry 3
	Key English Test (KET)	A2 (ALTE Level 1)	

* This represents the level typically required for employment purposes to signify the successful completion of compulsory secondary education in the UK.

BEC Preliminary

The BEC Preliminary examination consists of three papers:

Reading and Writing	1 hour 30 minutes
Listening	40 minutes (approximately)
Speaking	12 minutes

Introduction

Test of Reading and Writing (1 hour 30 minutes)

The **Reading** section of the Reading and Writing paper consists of seven parts with 45 questions, which take the form of two multiple-matching tasks, four multiple-choice tasks, and a form-filling or note-completion task. Part 1 contains five very short texts, Part 2 contains one short text, and Part 3 contains graphs, charts or tables. Parts 4, 5 and 6 each contain one longer text. Part 7 contains two short texts. The texts are mainly taken from newspapers, business magazines, business correspondence, books, leaflets, brochures, etc. They are all business-related, and are selected to test a wide range of reading skills and strategies.

For the **Writing** section of the Reading and Writing paper, candidates are required to produce two pieces of writing. For Part 1, they write a note, message, memo or email to a colleague or colleagues within the company. For Part 2, they write a piece of business correspondence to somebody outside the company. Candidates are asked to write 30 to 40 words for Part 1 and 60 to 80 words for Part 2. For Part 1, assessment is based on achievement of task. For Part 2, assessment is based on achievement of task, range and accuracy of vocabulary and grammatical structures, organisation, content, and appropriacy of register and format.

Test of Listening (approximately 40 minutes)

This paper consists of four parts with 30 questions, which take the form of two multiple-choice tasks and two note-completion tasks. Part 1 contains eight very short conversations or monologues, Part 2 contains a short conversation or monologue, Part 3 contains a monologue, and Part 4 contains one longer text. The texts are audio recordings based on a variety of sources including interviews, telephone calls, face-to-face conversations and documentary features. They are all business-related, and are selected to test a wide range of listening skills and strategies.

Test of Speaking (12 minutes)

The Speaking test consists of three parts, which take the form of an interview section, a short presentation on a business topic, and a discussion. In the standard test format, candidates are examined in pairs by two examiners: an interlocutor and an assessor. The assessor awards a mark based on the following four criteria: Grammar and Vocabulary, Discourse Management, Pronunciation and Interactive Communication. The interlocutor provides a global mark for the whole test.

Marks and results

The three BEC Preliminary papers total 120 marks, after weighting. Each skill (Reading, Writing, Listening and Speaking) is weighted to 30 marks.
A candidate's overall grade is based on the total score gained in all three papers. It is not necessary to achieve a satisfactory level in all three papers in order to pass the examination. Pass grades are Pass with Merit and Pass. The minimum successful performance in order to achieve a Pass corresponds to about 65% of the total marks. Narrow Fail and Fail are failing grades. Every candidate is

provided with a Statement of Results, which includes a graphical display of their performance in each skill. These are shown against the scale Exceptional – Good – Borderline – Weak and indicate the candidate's relative performance in each paper.

TO THE TEACHER

Candidature

Each year BEC is taken by over 120,000 candidates throughout the world. Most candidates are either already in work or studying in preparation for the world of work.

Content, preparation and assessment

Material used throughout BEC is as far as possible authentic and free of bias, and reflects the international flavour of the examination. The subject matter should not advantage or disadvantage certain groups of candidates, nor should it offend in areas such as religion, politics or sex.

TEST OF READING

Part	Main Skill Focus	Input	Response	No. of Questions
1	Reading – understanding short, real-world notices, messages, etc.	Notices, messages, timetables, adverts, leaflets, etc.	Multiple choice	5
2	Reading – detailed comprehension of factual material; skimming and scanning skills	Notice, list, plan, contents page, etc.	Matching	5
3	Reading – interpreting visual information	Graphs, charts, tables, etc. (The information may be presented in eight separate graphics or combined into a composite graphic.)	Matching	5
4	Reading for detailed factual information	Longer text (approx. 150–200 words): article, business letter, product description, report, minutes, etc.	Right/Wrong/ Doesn't say	7
5	Reading for gist and specific information	Longer text (approx. 300–400 words): newspaper or magazine article, advert, report, leaflet, etc.	Multiple choice	6
6	Reading – grammatical accuracy and understanding of text structure	Longer text (approx. 125–150 words): newspaper or magazine article, advert, leaflet, etc.	Multiple-choice cloze	12
7	Reading and information transfer	Short memos, letters, notices, adverts, etc.	Form-filling, note completion	5

Introduction

Reading Part One

In this part there are five short texts, each of which is accompanied by a multiple-choice question containing three options. In all cases the information will be brief and clear and the difficulty of the task will lie not in understanding context but in identifying or interpreting meaning.

A wide variety of text types, representative of the world of international business, can appear in this part. Each text will be complete and have a recognisable context.

Preparation
In order to prepare for this part, it would be useful to expose students to a wide range of notices and short texts taken from business settings. It is also useful to practise answering sample questions, asking students to explain why the answer is correct (and why the two incorrect options do not apply).

Reading Part Two

This is a matching task comprising one text and five questions, which are often descriptions of people's requirements. Candidates are required to match each question to an appropriate part of the text labelled A–H. (As there are only five questions, some of the labels are redundant.) The testing focus of this part is vocabulary and meaning.

Preparation
For preparation purposes, students need to be familiar with text types that are divided into lists, headings or categories; for example, the contents page of a directory or book, the plan of an office, the departments in a business or shop, or the items in a catalogue. Many of the questions in this part require a simple interpretation of what the parts of the text mean, and preparation for this could involve setting students real-world tasks of this kind using authentic (but simple) sources.

Reading Part Three

This task consists of eight graphs or charts (or one or more charts or graphs with eight distinct elements) and five questions. Each question is a description of a particular visual, and candidates are expected to match the questions to their corresponding graphs, which are labelled A–H.

Preparation
This part focuses on understanding trends and changes. Candidates need to be able to interpret graphic data and understand the language used to describe it. Expressions such as 'rose steadily', 'remained stable', 'decreased slowly' and 'reached a peak' should be introduced to students, along with relevant topics, such as sales of goods, share price movement and monthly costs.

Reading Part Four

This task is a text accompanied by seven, three-option multiple-choice items. Each question presents a statement, and candidates are expected to indicate whether the statement is A 'Right' or B 'Wrong' according to the text, or whether the information is not given in the text (C 'Doesn't say'). Candidates will not be expected to understand every word in the text but they should be able to pick out salient points and infer meaning where words in the text are unfamiliar. The questions will refer to factual information in the text but candidates will be required to do some processing in order to answer the questions correctly.

Preparation
This can be a difficult task for candidates who are not familiar with the three choices represented by A, B and C, and who might not understand the difference between a statement that is incorrect and one that depends on information that is not provided in the text. Students need to be trained to identify a false statement, which means that the opposite or a contradictory statement is made in the text, and to recognise that this is not the same as a statement that is not covered in the text (for which an alternative answer might be 'Don't know').

Reading Part Five

This part presents a single text accompanied by six multiple-choice comprehension items. The text is informative and is often taken from a leaflet, or from a newspaper or magazine article.

Candidates are expected to employ more complex reading strategies in this task, in that they should demonstrate their ability to extract relevant information, to read for gist and detail, to scan the text for specific information, and to understand the purpose of the writer and the audience for which the text is intended.

Preparation
In preparing candidates for this part, it would be a good idea to expose them to a variety of texts of a similar length. As texts become longer, slow readers are at a disadvantage and some practice in improving reading speed would be beneficial for this part. It would also be useful to discuss the following areas:
- the title
- the topic
- the writer's purpose
- the theme or main idea of each paragraph
- factual details that can be found in the text
- the writer's opinions (if they are evident).

Reading Part Six

This is a multiple-choice cloze test. Candidates have to select the correct word from three options to complete twelve gaps. This part has a predominantly grammatical focus and tests candidates' understanding of the general and detailed meaning of a text and in particular their ability to analyse structural patterns.

Introduction

Preparation

Any practice in the grammatical and structural aspects of the language is useful in preparing students for this part. However, it is equally important for students to analyse the structure and coherence of language within longer discourse so that they are encouraged to read for meaning beyond the sentence level. As tasks such as this typically focus on common grammatical difficulties, it it also useful to ask students to analyse the errors in their own work. Pairwork activities might be productive as students can often help each other in the areas of error identification and analysis.

Reading Part Seven

Candidates are given two short texts, for example a memo and an advertisement, and are asked to complete a form based on this material. There are five gaps, which should be completed with a word, a number or a short phrase. In this part, candidates are tested on their ability to extract relevant information and complete a form accurately.

For this part, candidates need to transfer their answers in capital letters to an Answer Sheet.

Marks

One mark is given for each correct answer. The total score for Reading is then weighted to 30 marks.

TEST OF WRITING

Part	Functions/Communicative Task	Input	Response	Register
1	e.g. (re-)arranging appointments, asking for permission, giving instructions	Rubric only (plus layout of output text type)	Internal communication (medium may be note, message, memo or email) (30–40 words)	Neutral/ formal/ informal
2	e.g. apologising and offering compensation, making or altering reservations, dealing with requests, giving information about a product	One piece of input, which may be business correspondence (medium may be letter, fax or email), internal communication (medium may be note, memo or email), notice, advert, etc. (plus layout of output text type)	Business correspondence (medium may be letter, fax or email) (60–80 words)	Neutral/ formal

For BEC Preliminary, candidates are required to produce two pieces of writing:
- an internal company communication; this means a piece of communication with a colleague or colleagues within the company on a business-related matter, and the delivery medium may be a note, message, memo or email;

Introduction

- a piece of business correspondence; this means correspondence with somebody outside the company (e.g. a customer or supplier) on a business-related matter, and the delivery medium may be a letter, fax or email.

Writing Part One

Candidates are asked to produce a concise piece of internal company communication of between 30 and 40 words, using a written prompt. The text will need to be produced in the form of a note, message, memo or email, and candidates are given guidance on the layout of memos and emails. The reason for writing and target reader are specified in the rubric, and bullet points explain what content points have to be included. Relevant ideas for one or more of these points will have to be 'invented' by the candidate.

Writing Part Two

Candidates are asked to produce an extended piece of business correspondence of between 60 and 80 words. This task involves the processing of a short text, such as a letter or advertisement, in order to respond to it. A number of bulleted content points below the text clearly indicate what should be included in the answer. Some of this information will need to be 'invented' by the candidate.

Although the use of some key words is inevitable, candidates should not 'lift' phrases from the question paper to use in their answers. This may be penalised.

Preparing for the Writing questions

In preparing students for the Writing tasks, it would be beneficial to familiarise them with a variety of business correspondence. Analysing authentic correspondence would help students understand better how to structure their answer and the type of language to use. When doing this, it would be useful to focus on the following areas:
- the purpose of the correspondence
- references to previous communication
- factual details
- the feelings and attitude of the writer
- the level of formality
- the opening sentence
- the closing sentence
- paragraphing
- the desired outcome.

If students are in a class, it might be possible to ask them to write and reply to each other's correspondence so that they can appreciate the importance of accurate content.

In a similar fashion, internal company memos and messages might also be written and analysed in terms of the above so that students can recognise the different levels of formality involved. It is a necessary part of preparing for the test that students understand the uses of, and styles inherent in, different types of business communication so that they are aware of how and why different types of correspondence are used.

Introduction

Assessment

An impression mark is awarded to each piece of writing. The General Impression Mark Scheme is used in conjunction with a task-specific mark scheme, which focuses on criteria specific to each particular task. This summarises the content, organisation, register, format and target reader indicated in the task.

For Part 1, examiners use the mark schemes primarily to assess task achievement. For Part 2, examiners use the mark schemes to assess both task achievement **and** language.

The band scores awarded are translated to a mark out of 5 for Part 1 and a mark out of 10 for Part 2. The total score for Writing is then weighted to 30 marks.

Both General Impression Mark Schemes are interpreted at Council of Europe Level B1.

Summaries of the General Impression Mark Schemes are reproduced below. Examiners work with a more detailed version, which is subject to regular updating.

General Impression Mark Scheme for Writing Part One

Band	
5	**Very good attempt** at task, achieving all content points.
4	**Good attempt** at task, achieving all content points.
3	**Satisfactory attempt** at task, achieving all content points with some effort by the reader, or achieving two content points.
2	**Inadequate attempt** at task, achieving one content point, possibly with noticeable irrelevance.
1	**Poor attempt** at task; no content points achieved, has little relevance.
0	No relevant response or too little language to assess.

General Impression Mark Scheme for Writing Part Two

Band	
5	Full realisation of the task set. • All four content points achieved. • Confident and ambitious use of language; errors are minor, due to ambition, and non-impeding. • Good range of structures and vocabulary. • Effectively organised, with appropriate use of simple linking devices. • Register and format consistently appropriate. Very positive effect on the reader.
4	Good realisation of the task set. • Three or four content points achieved. • Ambitious use of language; some non-impeding errors. • More than adequate range of structures and vocabulary. • Generally well organised, with attention paid to cohesion. • Register and format on the whole appropriate. Positive effect on the reader.
3	Reasonable achievement of the task set. • Three content points achieved. • A number of errors may be present, but are mostly non-impeding. • Adequate range of structures and vocabulary. • Organisation and cohesion are satisfactory, on the whole. • Register and format reasonable, although not entirely successful. Satisfactory effect on the reader.
2	Inadequate attempt at the task set. • Two or three content points achieved. • Numerous errors, which sometimes impede communication. • Limited range of structures and vocabulary. • Content is not clearly organised or linked, causing some confusion. • Inappropriate register and format. Negative effect on the reader.
1	Poor attempt at the task set. • One or two content points achieved. • Serious lack of control; frequent basic errors. • Little evidence of structures and vocabulary required by task. • Lack of organisation, causing a breakdown in communication. • Little attempt at appropriate register and format. Very negative effect on the reader.
0	Achieves nothing. Either fewer than 25% of the required number of words or totally illegible or totally irrelevant.

Introduction

TEST OF LISTENING

Part	Main Skill Focus	Input	Response	No. of Questions
1	Listening for specific information	Short conversations/ monologues	3-option multiple choice	8
2	Listening for specific information	Short telephone conversation/ prompted monologue	Gap-filling (numbers and spellings)	7
3	Listening for specific information	Monologue	Note-taking (content words)	7
4	Listening for gist/specific information	Conversation/interview/ discussion between two or more people	3-option multiple choice	8

Listening Part One

The eight questions in this part of the paper are three-option multiple-choice questions. For each question, candidates hear a short conversation or monologue, typically lasting around 15 to 30 seconds. Each monologue or dialogue is repeated on the recording in order to give candidates a chance to check their answer. The multiple-choice options may be textual or they may be in the form of pictures, graphs or diagrams.

In the extracts in Part 1, candidates are being tested on their understanding of spoken English used in a range of situations and on their ability to extract factual information. They may need to pick out a name or time or place. Alternatively, they may have to identify a trend in a graph or a place on a map or the location of an object in a room. In every case, it will be necessary for candidates to follow the conversation closely.

Listening Part Two

This part consists of a short conversation or monologue, typically lasting around a minute and a half, which contains factual information. On the question paper there is a form, table, chart or set of notes with seven gaps where information is missing. Candidates have to complete each of the gaps. This part has a numerical focus and the answers may include dates, prices, percentages or figures.

Listening Part Three

Candidates hear a monologue. On the question paper there is a set of notes or a form with gaps. There are seven gaps to complete and the answers may be one or two words. On occasion, the key to one of the gaps may be a date.

Listening Part Four

This part, which lasts about three minutes, contains a longer listening text which generally takes the form of an interview, or a discussion between two or possibly more speakers. There are eight three-option multiple-choice questions on the question paper and these are always in a written format. In this part of the Listening component, candidates are being tested on their ability to understand the gist of a longer text and extract detailed and specific information as required by the questions. They may also be tested on the speakers' opinions.

At the end of the Listening test, candidates have ten minutes to transfer their answers to their Answer Sheet.

Preparing for the Listening paper

The Listening component is carefully paced and candidates are tested on short extracts in Part 1, so that they can gradually 'tune in' to the spoken language and improve their listening skills without losing their place in the test.

Listening can be a very demanding activity, and candidates should practise their listening skills regularly using a wide variety of listening sources. Candidates who enter the Listening test having done this will be at an advantage.

At BEC Preliminary level, it is advisable to collect as much listening material as possible that is suitably paced and of an appropriate length. Native speakers speak at many different speeds and some speak much more clearly than others. If it is possible to collect a bank of authentic material that is carefully chosen, this would prove useful practice for students. Otherwise, it might be better to make use of specially designed materials for this level.

For Part 1, candidates should try to listen to short extracts of speech, concentrating on understanding the general idea or main points of what is said. For Parts 2 and 3, practice should be given in note-taking. Prior to hearing tapes or audio materials, students should be given details of the information they need to listen for. Teachers should discuss the task with the students beforehand and encourage them to listen for cues and prompts that will help them identify the points they need to find. When listening to longer texts, it would also be useful to discuss areas such as:
- the purpose of the speech or conversation
- the speakers' roles
- the speakers' opinions
- the language functions being used
- factual details
- conclusions.

Marks

One mark is given for each correct answer, giving a total score of 30 marks for the whole Listening paper.

Introduction

TEST OF SPEAKING

Part	Format/Content	Time	Interaction Focus
1	Conversation between the interlocutor and each candidate General interaction and social language	About 2 minutes	The interlocutor encourages the candidates to give information about themselves and to express personal opinions.
2	A 'mini presentation' by each candidate on a business theme Organising a larger unit of discourse Giving information and expressing opinions	About 5 minutes	Each candidate is given prompts which they use to prepare and give a short talk on a business-related topic.
3	Two-way conversation between candidates followed by further prompting from the interlocutor Expressing opinions, agreeing and disagreeing	About 5 minutes	The candidates are presented with a scenario supported by visual or written prompts which generates a discussion. The interlocutor extends the discussion with further spoken prompts.

The Speaking test is conducted by two oral examiners (an interlocutor and an assessor), with pairs of candidates. The interlocutor is responsible for conducting the Speaking test and is also required to give a mark for each candidate's performance during the whole test. The assessor is reponsible for providing an analytical assessment of each candidate's performance and, after being introduced by the interlocutor, takes no further part in the interaction.

The Speaking test is designed for pairs of candidates. However, where a centre has an uneven number of candidates, the last three candidates will be examined together.

Speaking Part One

In the first part of the test, the interlocutor addresses each candidate in turn and asks questions about where they work or study, where they live or what they do in their free time. The questions will be slightly different for each candidate, and candidates will not be addressed in strict sequence. This part of the test takes about two minutes and during this time candidates are tested on their ability to talk briefly about themselves, to provide information on subjects such as their home, hobbies and jobs, and to perform simple functions such as agreeing and disagreeing, and expressing preferences.

Speaking Part Two

The second part of the test is a 'mini presentation'. Candidates are asked to speak for about one minute on a business-related topic. At Preliminary level, candidates are given two topics from which they should choose **one**. Each topic is presented as a main focus with three bullet points. Candidates are given one minute to prepare the talk (both candidates or group of three prepare at the same time). After each candidate finishes speaking, the next candidate is asked which of the bullet points they think is the most important. This part of the test focuses on the candidate's ability to present basic ideas and organise a longer piece of discourse.

Speaking Part Three

The third part of the test is a discussion between candidates. The interlocutor outlines a scenario and provides prompts by way of black and white pictures or written prompts to help the candidates. The candidates are asked to speak for about two minutes. The interlocutor will support the conversation as appropriate and then ask further questions related to the main theme. This part of the test focuses on the candidate's ability to interact appropriately using a range of linguistic skills.

Preparing for the Speaking test

It is important to familiarise candidates with the format of the test before it takes place, by the use of paired activities in class. Teachers may need to explain the benefits of this type of assessment to candidates. The primary purpose of paired assessment is to sample a wider range of discourse than can be elicited from an individual interview.

In the first part of the test, candidates mainly respond to questions or comments from the interlocutor. In the second part, candidates are given the opportunity to produce an extended piece of discourse and to demonstrate an ability to maintain a longer speech turn. In the third part, they are required to interact more actively, taking turns appropriately, asking and answering questions and negotiating meaning. To prepare for this part, it is a good idea to encourage students to change partners in class so that they grow accustomed to interacting with a variety of people, some of whom they do not know so well.

For all parts of the test, students need to practise the exchange of personal and non-personal information, and prompt materials will be needed to help them do this. Teachers could prepare a selection of these for each part of the test. Students could discuss the materials as a class group prior to engaging in pairwork activities. Such activities would familiarise students with the types of interactive skills involved in asking and providing factual information, such as: speaking clearly, formulating questions, listening carefully and giving precise answers.

Assessment

Candidates are assessed on their own performance and not in relation to each other according to the following analytical criteria: Grammar and Vocabulary, Discourse Management, Pronunciation and Interactive Communication. These criteria are interpreted at Preliminary level. Assessment is based on performance in the whole test and is not related to particular parts of the test.

Introduction

Both examiners assess the candidates. The assessor applies detailed analytical scales, and the interlocutor applies a Global Achievement Scale, which is based on the analytical scales. The analytical criteria are further described below.

Grammar and Vocabulary

This refers to range and accuracy as well as the appropriate use of grammatical and lexical forms. At BEC Preliminary level, a range of grammar and vocabulary is needed to deal with the tasks. At this level, candidates may make frequent minor errors and use some inappropriate vocabulary, but this should not obscure intended meanings.

Discourse Management

This refers to the coherence, extent and relevance of each candidate's individual performance. Contributions should be adequate to deal with the BEC Preliminary level tasks.

Pronunciation

This refers to the candidate's ability to produce comprehensible utterances. At BEC Preliminary level, most meanings are conveyed through the appropriate use of stress, rhythm, intonation and clear individual sounds.

Interactive Communication

This refers to the candidate's ability to take an active part in the development of the discourse. At BEC Preliminary level, candidates are able to take turns and sustain the interaction by initiating and responding appropriately.

Global Achievement Scale

This refers to the candidate's overall performance throughout the test. Throughout the Speaking test, candidates are assessed on their language skills and, in order to be able to make a fair and accurate assessment of each candidate's performance, the examiners must be given an adequate sample of language to assess. Candidates must, therefore, be prepared to provide full answers to the questions asked by either the interlocutor or the other candidate, and to speak clearly and audibly. While it is the responsibility of the interlocutor, where necessary, to manage or direct the interaction, thus ensuring that both candidates are given an equal opportunity to speak, it is the responsibility of the candidates to maintain the interaction as much as possible.

Grading and results

Grading takes place once all scripts have been returned to Cambridge ESOL and marking is complete. This is approximately five weeks after the examination. There are two main stages: grading and awards.

Grading

The three papers total 120 marks, after weighting. Each skill represents 25% of the total marks available. The grade boundaries (Pass with Merit, Pass, Narrow Fail and Fail) are set using the following information:
- statistics on the candidature
- statistics on the overall candidate performance
- statistics on individual items, for those parts of the examination for which this is appropriate (Reading and Listening)
- the advice of the Principal Examiners, based on the performance of candidates, and on the recommendation of examiners where this is relevant (Writing)
- comparison with statistics from previous years' examination performance and candidature.

A candidate's overall grade is based on the total score gained in all three papers. It is not necessary to achieve a satisfactory level in all three papers in order to pass the examination.

Awards

The Awarding Committee deals with all cases presented for special consideration, e.g. temporary disability, unsatisfactory examination conditions, suspected collusion, etc. The Committee can decide to ask for scripts to be re-marked, to check results, to change grades, to withhold results, etc. Results may be withheld because of infringement of regulations or because further investigation is needed. Centres are notified if a candidate's results have been scrutinised by the Awarding Committee.

Results

Results are reported as two passing grades (Pass with Merit and Pass) and two failing grades (Narrow Fail and Fail). The minimum successful performance which a candidate typically requires in order to achieve a Pass corresponds to about 65% of the total marks. Candidates are given a Statement of Results which, in addition to their grades, shows a graphical profile of their performance on each paper. These are shown against the scale Exceptional – Good – Borderline – Weak and indicate the candidate's relative performance in each paper. Certificates are issued to passing candidates after the issue of the Statement of Results, and there is no limit on the validity of the certificates.

Further information

For more information about BEC or any other Cambridge ESOL examination, write to:

University of Cambridge ESOL Examinations
1 Hills Road
Cambridge CB1 2EU
United Kingdom

Tel: +44 1223 553997
Fax: +44 1223 553621
email: ESOLHelpdesk@ucles.org.uk
website: www.CambridgeESOL.org

In some areas, this information can also be obtained from the British Council.

Test 1

READING AND WRITING   1 hour 30 minutes

READING

PART ONE

Questions 1–5

- Look at questions **1–5**.
- In each question, which sentence is correct?
- For each question, mark one letter (**A**, **B** or **C**) on your Answer Sheet.

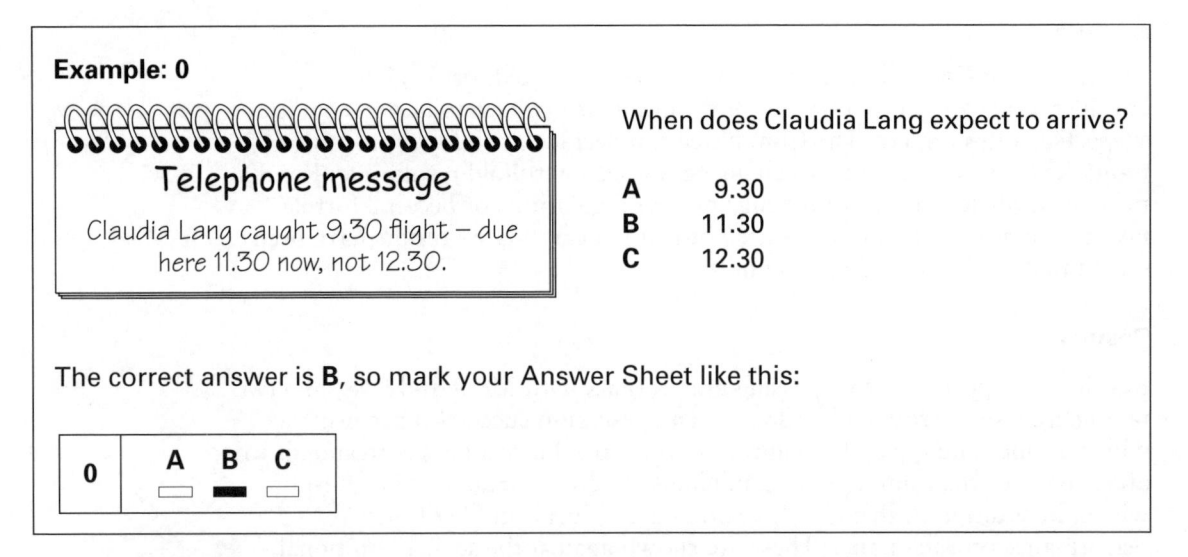

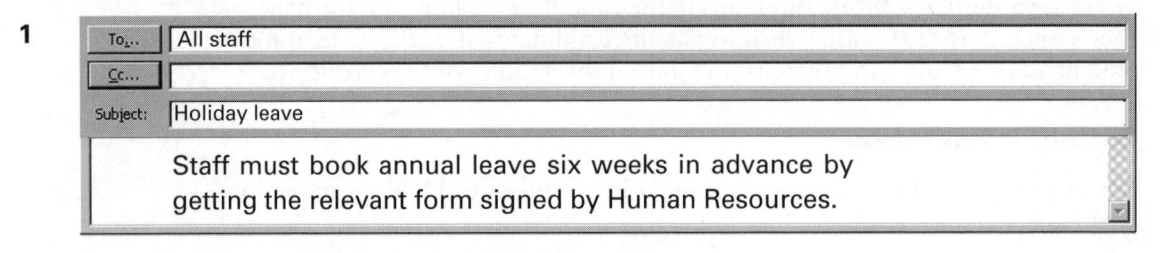

Example: 0

Telephone message

Claudia Lang caught 9.30 flight – due here 11.30 now, not 12.30.

When does Claudia Lang expect to arrive?

A   9.30
B   11.30
C   12.30

The correct answer is **B**, so mark your Answer Sheet like this:

| 0 | A | B | C |

1

To... All staff
Cc...
Subject: Holiday leave

Staff must book annual leave six weeks in advance by getting the relevant form signed by Human Resources.

A   Staff are allowed six weeks' holiday a year.
B   Staff must book holidays before the end of the year.
C   Staff must have their holiday requests approved.

2

> **Information for customers**
>
> All goods transported by Fera Carriers are insured, but our policy excludes damage due to poor packaging.

A   Customers will not necessarily qualify for compensation if goods are damaged.
B   Customers should arrange insurance against damage before sending goods.
C   Customers are able to claim a refund if packaging is damaged.

3

> **MEMO**
>
> To: Wei Yu
> From: Human Resources
> Date: 18 November
> Subject: Training
>
> We can't say whether your training application will be accepted until we can confirm that funds are available.

A   Wei Yu should re-apply for his training course at a later date.
B   There may not be enough money to pay for Wei Yu's course.
C   Human Resources cannot confirm which training course Wei Yu should take.

4

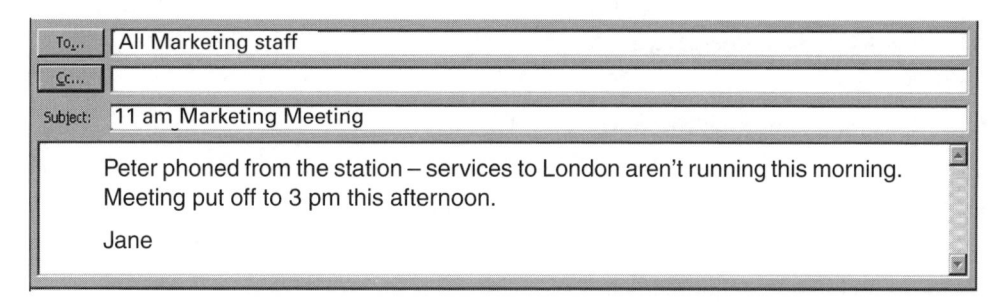

> To...: All Marketing staff
> Cc...:
> Subject: 11 am Marketing Meeting
>
> Peter phoned from the station – services to London aren't running this morning. Meeting put off to 3 pm this afternoon.
> Jane

A   The 11 am meeting is postponed because Peter's train was cancelled.
B   Peter will arrive at the 11 am meeting late because his train is delayed.
C   The 11 am meeting is rescheduled because Peter was late and missed his train.

5

> The safety team is carrying out checks in this area.
> Access without a permit is denied until further notice.

A   A permit is currently required for entry to this area.
B   Special care should be taken when entering this area.
C   Permission to enter this area can be obtained from safety staff.

Test 1

PART TWO

Questions 6–10

- Look at the advertisement below. It shows a list of workshops offered by a training company.
- For questions **6–10**, decide which workshop (**A–H**) each person on the opposite page should attend.
- For each question, mark one letter (**A–H**) on your Answer Sheet.
- Do not use any letter more than once.

WORKSHOPS

A Classifying consumers

B Communications with customers

C Factors in setting pricing levels

D How to encourage repeat business

E Making a cashflow forecast

F Measuring consumer response to marketing

G Producing financial statements of past performance

H Researching potential markets

6 Julia Strekalova wants to know how to calculate the amount she can charge customers for her marketing consultancy services.

7 Roger Walker's company wants to give him responsibility for his firm's annual profit-and-loss account and balance sheet.

8 Paolo Longo needs to be able to assess the effect on sales following his company's recent product promotions.

9 Zhon Mei Feng's company wants her to learn to divide the market into groups, which it can target with different brands.

10 Valerija Georgievska needs a course on working out how much money her firm can expect to have available each month.

Test 1

PART THREE

Questions 11–15

- Look at the chart below. It shows a company's turnover, operating profit and market share over a period of ten months.
- Which month does each sentence (**11–15**) on the opposite page describe?
- For each sentence, mark one letter (**A–H**) on your Answer Sheet.
- Do not use any letter more than once.

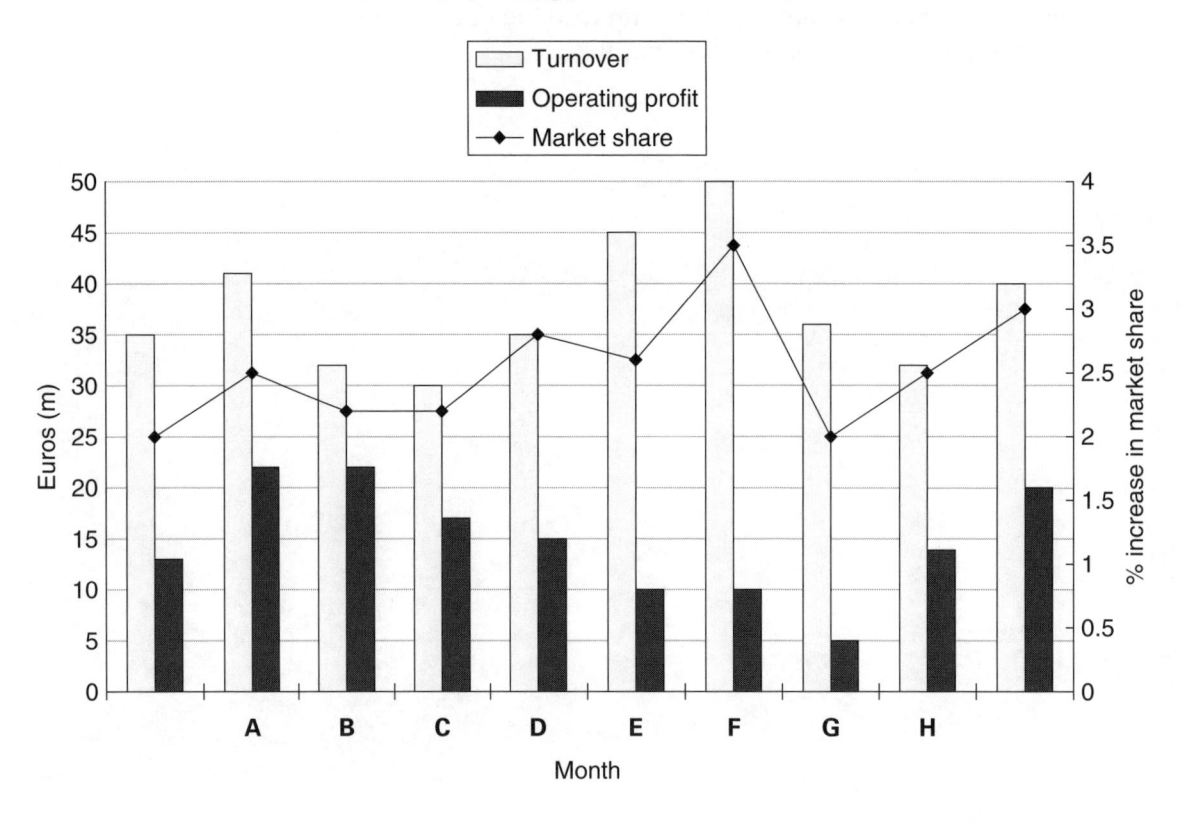

Turnover, operating profit and market share

11 Although operating profit dropped and market share experienced a decline, there was an upturn in the level of turnover.

12 Both turnover and market share showed an increase this month, while operating profit suffered a decline.

13 Despite the fact that market share fell and there was a decline in turnover, operating profit was equal to that of the previous month.

14 While turnover experienced a downturn, both operating profit and market share showed signs of recovery.

15 Although market share showed an improvement and turnover also increased, this had no effect on the month's operating profit.

PART FOUR

Questions 16–22

- Read the job advertisement below.
- Are sentences **16–22** on the opposite page 'Right' or 'Wrong'? If there is not enough information to answer 'Right' or 'Wrong', choose 'Doesn't say'.
- For each sentence (**16–22**), mark one letter (**A**, **B** or **C**) on your Answer Sheet.

Vacancies for Store Managers

Scene Video has been quietly successful in recent years, and we now have 23 stores worldwide – including 15 in Canada – with a further ten on the way. We are now offering exciting management opportunities.

As store manager, you'll have unusual independence – which will make most retail management posts seem easy compared with ours! You will be in charge of a store with over 40 staff, and you'll have a salary to match.

Whether you've worked in retail management or in another field involving customer relations, we want to hear from you. You'll be a strong leader, full of ideas and ambition, and commercially aware, preferably with knowledge of the retail industry in one of the countries where we have stores. If you are willing to relocate, you could be on track for fast promotion.

To find out what part you can play in our continuing success, you are invited to an informal Introductory Evening at any of our stores (details below). Or visit our website for more information and to download an application form. Please post this, together with a handwritten letter explaining why you are suited to the job.

16 Scene Video is planning to open more stores.

    A Right   **B** Wrong   **C** Doesn't say

17 Scene Video believes its store managers have a harder job than other store managers.

    A Right   **B** Wrong   **C** Doesn't say

18 Scene Video's salaries are higher than for similar positions in other retail businesses.

    A Right   **B** Wrong   **C** Doesn't say

19 It is essential for applicants to have experience as store managers.

    A Right   **B** Wrong   **C** Doesn't say

20 Most successful applicants will have to spend time working in different countries.

    A Right   **B** Wrong   **C** Doesn't say

21 The Introductory Evenings are targeted at successful candidates.

    A Right   **B** Wrong   **C** Doesn't say

22 Application forms should be completed online.

    A Right   **B** Wrong   **C** Doesn't say

PART FIVE

Questions 23–28

- Read the article below about a successful business partnership.
- For each question (23–28) on the opposite page, choose the correct answer.
- Mark one letter (**A, B** or **C**) on your Answer Sheet.

PARTNERS IN SUCCESS

Phil Brook and Sean Williams are friends who set up a company in 1997 providing finance to companies making IT purchases. Their firm, Syscap, now turns over £120m a year.

'I'm an extrovert, so selling fits my character,' explains Phil Brook. 'I started selling photocopiers, and it didn't take me long to achieve the agreed sales targets. Then, in 1994, I realised the IT industry was about to explode, and I decided to try and sell IT. I met a guy who was setting up as a computer re-seller, and I worked for him for three years, expanding his company to a turnover of £3–£4m. We were among only a few people selling computer systems on lease, so we were attractive to reps offering finance. There was this guy from CTL Bank called Sean Williams who rang us dozens of times, trying to sell me IT finance. I was already getting finance from somebody else, but he kept on calling. That impressed me – I thought, if he's any good, maybe I'll recruit him.'

Sean Williams adds, 'When we finally met, we went out to lunch and became firm friends. I thought Phil was fun, and we had similar interests. The next day, we did a deal together, and I provided him with all the finance he needed. Then he realised, and I soon agreed, that there was a big opportunity to do independently what I was already doing for the bank. So he left his job and established Syscap. It took me a while to decide to join him, because I was among the top salespeople nationally at my bank, and my future was planned. But I knew when I did that it was the right decision. I knew we had the same ideas about work. When you work hard, you get there, whether you're good or not. It's like golf. The more you practise, the luckier you get. With us, the more times we picked up the phone, the more deals we made. The business soon took off enormously. I've always had big ambitions, but I didn't expect it to become as big as this.'

Phil thinks that the next few years look promising. 'The competition in this trade is weak,' he says, 'so I believe we can turn this into a £1bn company. People in our industry find it amazing that Sean and I still get on so well after all this time. But I'm glad we do. It's our partnership that makes the job fun.'

23 Phil stopped selling photocopiers because he

   A   was unable to meet the sales targets.
   B   recognised an opportunity in another field.
   C   became aware of their limited market potential.

24 Why did Phil agree to meet Sean?

   A   He liked the way Sean did not give up trying.
   B   He thought they would have a lot of common interests.
   C   He needed someone to provide IT finance for his clients.

25 Why did Sean not join Phil immediately at Syscap?

   A   He had doubts about the profitability of the venture.
   B   He was unsure about giving up an established career.
   C   He was afraid that working together would damage their friendship.

26 In what way does Sean believe that business is like golf?

   A   You cannot achieve your goals without taking risks.
   B   To do well, you need a combination of ability and ambition.
   C   If you do something enough times, you'll eventually be successful.

27 Sean says he is surprised that

   A   he and Phil are still good friends.
   B   their company has been so successful.
   C   more people do not set up their own businesses.

28 What makes Phil confident about their company's future growth?

   A   the strength of the friendship they have
   B   being in a commercial field which is rapidly expanding
   C   having few serious challengers for their position in the marketplace

Test 1

PART SIX

Questions 29–40

- Read the introduction to a company report below.
- Choose the correct word to fill each gap from **A, B** or **C** on the opposite page.
- For each question (**29–40**), mark one letter (**A, B** or **C**) on your Answer Sheet.

GLOBAL CHALLENGES, LOCAL ACTIONS

Every day around the world, 150 million people choose our products. They buy them **(29)** .... that they can feed their families and keep their homes clean. By making and selling brands that **(30)** .... people's everyday needs, we have **(31)** .... into one of the world's largest consumer goods businesses.

We believe that the very business of '**(32)** .... business' in a responsible way **(33)** .... positive social effects. We not **(34)** .... create wealth, we also share it. As **(35)** .... global company, we play our part **(36)** .... addressing global social and environmental concerns such as health and hygiene, and water quality.

However, we do not believe **(37)** .... is practical to respond to these concerns purely **(38)** .... an international level. Nor do we believe that our company can make a difference **(39)** .... working in a number of partnerships. That is **(40)** .... we work together with local agencies and governments.

29	A	as	B	although	C	so
30	A	join	B	catch	C	meet
31	A	grown	B	risen	C	increased
32	A	do	B	doing	C	done
33	A	has	B	gets	C	takes
34	A	even	B	just	C	only
35	A	the	B	a	C	this
36	A	on	B	for	C	in
37	A	there	B	it	C	what
38	A	at	B	with	C	of
39	A	until	B	except	C	without
40	A	whether	B	why	C	where

Test 1

PART SEVEN

Questions 41–45

- Read the email and memo below.
- Complete the form on the opposite page.
- Write a word or phrase (in CAPITAL LETTERS) or a number on lines **41–45** on your Answer Sheet.

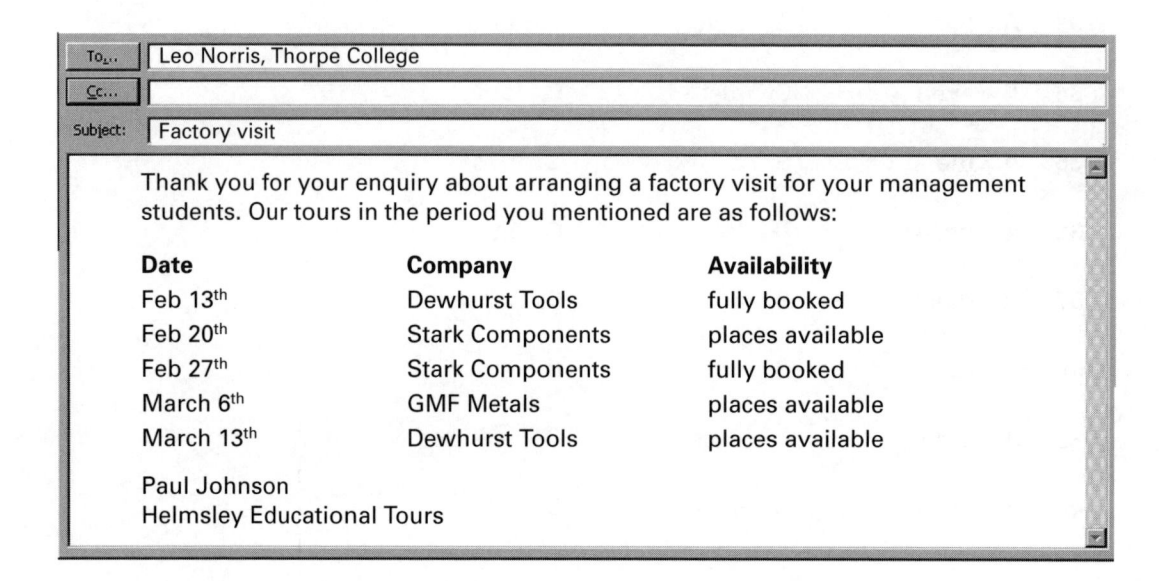

To...	Leo Norris, Thorpe College
Cc...	
Subject:	Factory visit

Thank you for your enquiry about arranging a factory visit for your management students. Our tours in the period you mentioned are as follows:

Date	Company	Availability
Feb 13th	Dewhurst Tools	fully booked
Feb 20th	Stark Components	places available
Feb 27th	Stark Components	fully booked
March 6th	GMF Metals	places available
March 13th	Dewhurst Tools	places available

Paul Johnson
Helmsley Educational Tours

MEMORANDUM
Thorpe College

To: Jan Partridge
From: Leo Norris
Date: November 18th
Subject: Factory visit

Jan – Could you book the earliest possible visit, please? We've got 15 on the management course next term, and of course either you or I will have to go too. Remember that we've got a guest speaker on Feb 20th, so that's out. As I'm on holiday soon, they'd better send information to you. The invoice should come to the Course Secretary before it goes to Accounts.

HELMSLEY EDUCATIONAL TOURS
Booking form

Organisation requesting tour: (**41**)   ....

Date of tour: (**42**)   ....

Total number of people: (**43**)   ....

Full name of contact person: (**44**)   ....

Invoice to be sent to: (**45**)   ....

Test 1

WRITING

PART ONE

Question 46

- Your department currently has a lot of work, and your secretary must take several weeks off work, starting tomorrow.
- Write an **email** to the Human Resources Manager in your company:
  - explaining why your department is so busy
  - saying why your secretary will be away from work
  - asking for a temporary secretary.
- Write **30–40** words on your Answer Sheet.

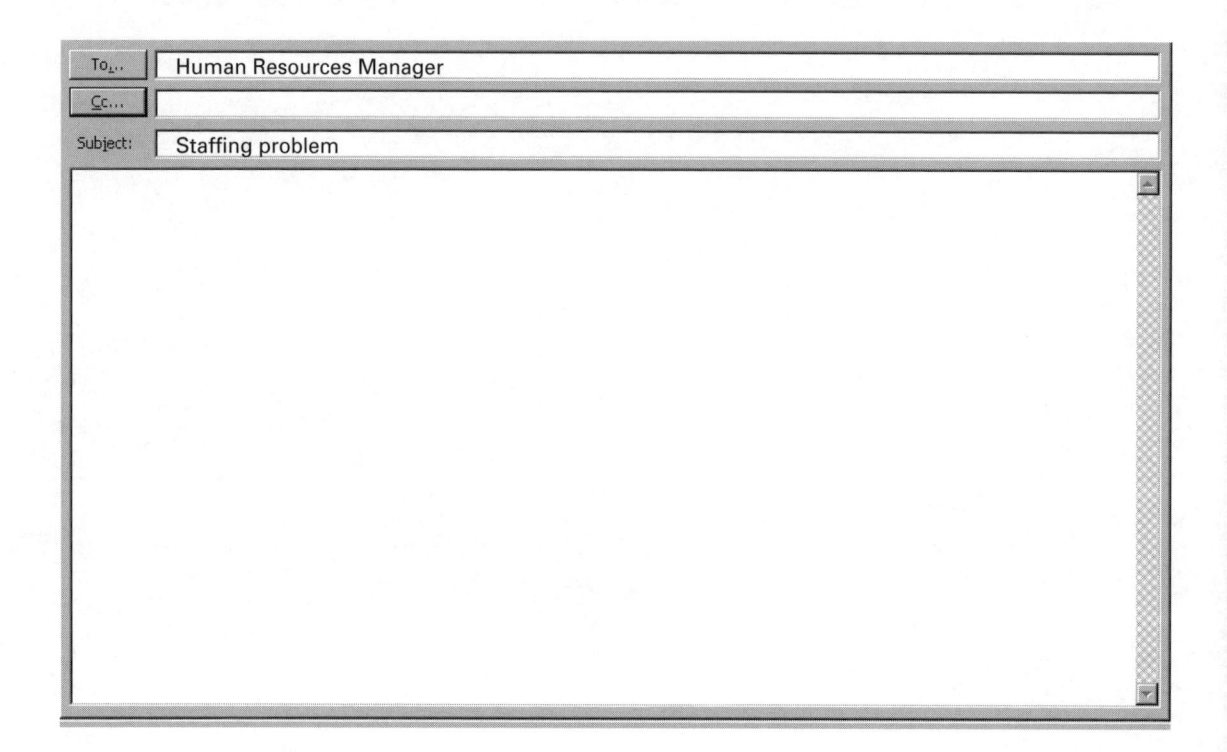

To...	Human Resources Manager
Cc...	
Subject:	Staffing problem

Writing

PART TWO

Question 47

- Read part of a letter below from a company which runs training courses for staff.

> We are an established company providing a wide range of training services for all kinds of business. We have our own purpose-built centre where we hold courses, or training can be offered at the client's own premises if preferred. We offer excellent value for money and a full 100% satisfaction guarantee.
>
> For further information, or to arrange an appointment to discuss your requirements, please contact Miss Jane Foster.

- Write an **email** to Miss Foster:
  - expressing an interest in her company's services
  - describing your company's training needs
  - explaining why your company's premises would be the most suitable place
  - inviting her to a meeting next week.
- Write **60–80** words on your Answer Sheet.
- Do not include any postal addresses.

Dear Miss Foster,

Test 1

LISTENING   Approximately 40 minutes (including 10 minutes' transfer time)

PART ONE

Questions 1–8

- For questions **1–8**, you will hear eight short recordings.
- For each question, mark **one** letter (**A**, **B** or **C**) for the correct answer.

> **Example:**
>
> Who is Emily going to write to?
>
> **A** the staff
> **B** the supplier
> **C** the clients
>
> The answer is **A**.

- After you have listened once, replay each recording.

1 What is the quotation for 1,000 brochures with colour photos?

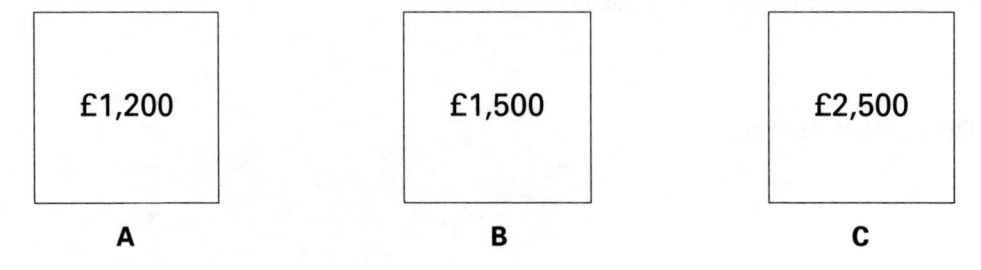

£1,200	£1,500	£2,500
A	B	C

2 When will the new Personnel Officer start work?

    A July
    B September
    C October

3 Which pie chart is correct?

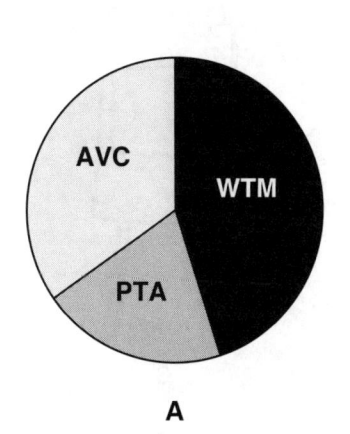

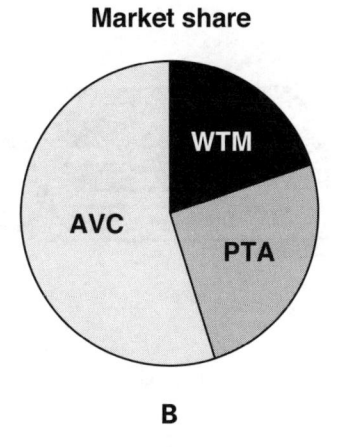

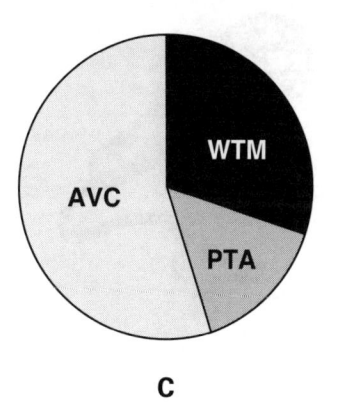

Market share

A B C

4 Why is Jane unhappy about Michael's report?

- **A** He has left mistakes in it.
- **B** He has finished it very late.
- **C** He has circulated it too soon.

5 What is the woman's current job with BGT?

- **A** Project Manager
- **B** General Manager
- **C** Account Manager

6 What does the speaker think the company should do?

- **A** increase online bookings
- **B** cut ticket prices
- **C** reduce spending on food

Test 1

7 What does the woman need to get?

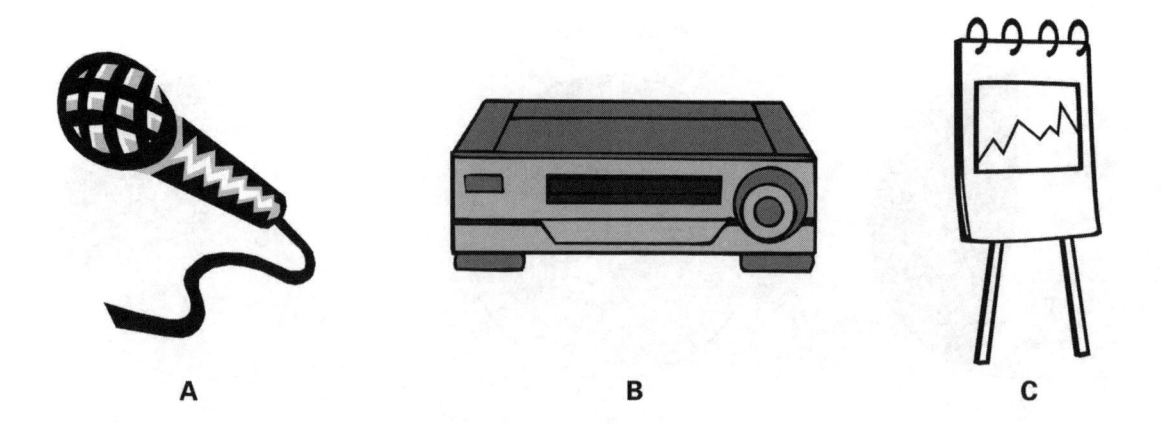

A   B   C

8 Which graph shows the company figures?

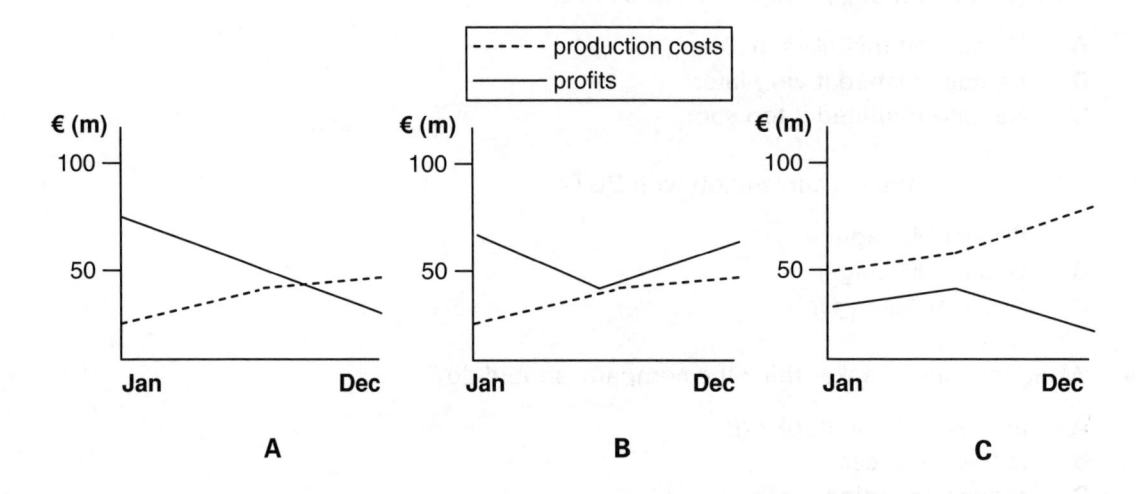

A   B   C

Listening

PART TWO

Questions 9–15

- Look at the notes below.
- Some information is missing.
- You will hear a man discussing an order from an office supply company.
- For each question (**9–15**), fill in the missing information in the numbered space using **a word**, **number** or **letters**.
- After you have listened once, replay the recording.

Wilson's Office Supplies

Customer Return

Customer name:	(9)	.... *International*
Invoice date:		*5th July*
Order number:	(10)	....
Item to be returned:		*Desk*
New order:		
Width required:	(11)	.... *cm*
Reference number:	(12)	....
Price including discount:	(13)	£ ....
Credit due:	(14)	£ ....
Delivery date:	(15)	.... *July*

Test 1

PART THREE

Questions 16–22

- Look at the notes below.
- Some information is missing.
- You will hear a man giving a presentation about Arlington Park, a training centre for managers.
- For each question (**16–22**), fill in the missing information in the numbered space using **one** or **two** words.
- After you have listened once, replay the recording.

ARLINGTON PARK

Every third Thursday there's an (16) ....

Titles of weekend workshops

  10th June: (17) ....

  17th July: (18) ....

Also offers three-day programmes with (19) ....

Facilities include training suites and a (20) ....

Name of Arlington Park magazine: (21) ....

To get on mailing list, complete (22) .... (leave at reception)

Listening

PART FOUR

Questions 23–30

- You will hear an interview with John Winterman, the Managing Director of a sports-equipment manufacturing company called Turners.
- For each question (**23–30**), mark **one** letter (**A**, **B** or **C**) for the correct answer.
- After you have listened once, replay the recording.

23 The managers at Turners wanted to buy the company because it

    A   was in a good state financially.
    B   made first-class products.
    C   had a strong brand image.

24 What particular problem did the previous owners leave behind at Turners?

    A   an unsuitable production system
    B   too wide a range of products
    C   a poor style of management

25 One problem with Turners' distribution process was the

    A   unreliable transportation system.
    B   product-numbering system.
    C   old-fashioned computer system.

26 What complaint did the sports outlets make?

    A   Deliveries were usually late.
    B   Goods were sometimes damaged.
    C   Orders were not complete.

27 Turners now intends to concentrate on promoting its products

    A   at big competitions.
    B   in schools.
    C   with sports clubs.

28 Which area of the company was re-organised first?

    A   manufacturing
    B   marketing
    C   finance

Test 1

29 The majority of Turners' manufacturing will soon be located in

    A Indonesia.
    B the Philippines.
    C Germany.

30 What is the company's main aim in product development?

    A introducing new designs
    B giving goods international appeal
    C improving existing lines

You now have 10 minutes to transfer your answers to your Answer Sheet.

SPEAKING   12 minutes

SAMPLE SPEAKING TASKS

PART ONE

In this part, the interlocutor asks questions to each of the candidates in turn. You have to give information about yourself and express personal opinions.

PART TWO

In this part of the test, you are asked to give a short talk on a business topic. You have to choose one of the topics from the two below and then talk for about one minute. You have one minute to prepare your ideas.

A: What is important when . . . ?

Arranging a social event for clients

- Types of activities
- Cost of event
- Giving presents

B: What is important when . . . ?

Choosing the location for a new factory

- Transport connections
- Cost
- Size of factory

Test 1

PART THREE

In this part of the test, the examiner reads out a scenario and gives you some prompt material in the form of pictures or words. You have 30 seconds to look at the task prompt, an example of which is below, and then about two minutes to discuss the scenario with your partner. After that, the examiner will ask you more questions related to the topic.

For **two** or **three** candidates

Scenario

> I'm going to describe a situation.
>
> **A large company is going to receive a two-day visit from a group of businesspeople from abroad. Talk together for about two minutes* about some of the things the visitors could do during their visit and decide how they will spend the first day.**
>
> Here are some ideas to help you.

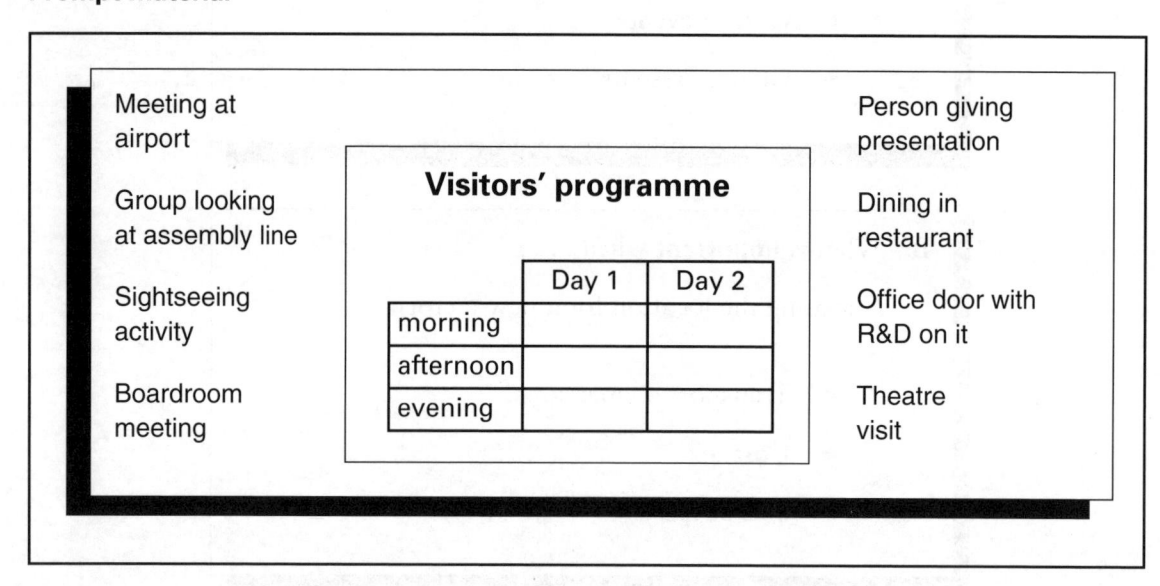

* three minutes for groups of three candidates

Prompt material

Meeting at airport

Group looking at assembly line

Sightseeing activity

Boardroom meeting

Person giving presentation

Dining in restaurant

Office door with R&D on it

Theatre visit

Visitors' programme

	Day 1	Day 2
morning		
afternoon		
evening		

Follow-on questions

- What other things could visitors to a company do?
- Why is it important to entertain company visitors?
- How can companies attract new customers?
- What kinds of things can companies do to keep their existing customers?
- Why is competition among companies sometimes a good thing?

Test 2

READING AND WRITING   1 hour 30 minutes

READING

PART ONE

Questions 1–5

- Look at questions **1–5**.
- In each question, which sentence is correct?
- For each question, mark one letter (**A**, **B** or **C**) on your Answer Sheet.

Example: 0

Telephone message

Claudia Lang caught 9.30 flight – due here 11.30 now, not 12.30.

When does Claudia Lang expect to arrive?

A   9.30
B   11.30
C   12.30

The correct answer is **B**, so mark your Answer Sheet like this:

0 A **B** C

1

Martin
Re: Soledad Ramirez's visit to March finance conference.
Hotel booking extended by one night as she has requested; location unchanged.
Bettina

Soledad Ramirez has asked

A   for a hotel closer to the conference centre.
B   to stay at the hotel longer than planned.
C   for confirmation that her conference accommodation is available.

Reading

2

> We may use your contact details to send to companies whose services may be of interest to you.

- **A** You are advised to contact a different company for the required information.
- **B** Your services could be of interest to a range of companies.
- **C** Some other companies might be given information about you.

3

> **Please note**
> Staff should contact the supplier's technicians if there is a fault and not attempt to repair the printer themselves.

Staff are expected to

- **A** try to fix minor faults with the printer.
- **B** report any faults with the printer.
- **C** inform their colleagues about faults with the printer.

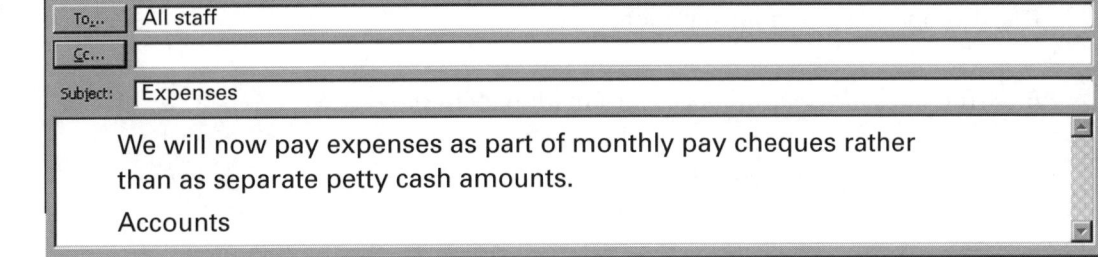

4

To...	All staff
Cc...	
Subject:	Expenses

We will now pay expenses as part of monthly pay cheques rather than as separate petty cash amounts.
Accounts

Staff will now receive expenses

- **A** monthly from petty cash.
- **B** along with their salaries.
- **C** as a separate cheque.

5

> **RETAIL NEWS**
> Marshalsea intends to launch its redesigned store look next year, depending on the success of trials this autumn.
> **CLICK HERE FOR FULL STORY**

- **A** As Marshalsea is satisfied with its trials, it will refurbish stores in the autumn.
- **B** Marshalsea hopes it will see improved results this autumn after refurbishing all its stores.
- **C** If Marshalsea is satisfied with the results of its experiments, stores will be refurbished.

Test 2

PART TWO

Questions 6–10

- Look at the list below. It shows the contents of a business magazine.
- For questions **6–10**, decide which section (**A–H**) would be most suitable for each person or company on the opposite page.
- For each question, mark one letter (**A–H**) on your Answer Sheet.
- Do not use any letter more than once.

IN THIS MONTH'S MAGAZINE . . .

A Mergers and acquisitions

B Making stores more attractive

C Recent moves to senior positions

D Comparing potential suppliers

E The latest developments in information technology

F How to improve productivity

G CV – this month's profile: a top financial manager

H Transferring central control of your business

6 The Chief Executive of a newly merged manufacturing company wishes to read about ideas for raising output without increasing costs.

7 A retail chain's senior management want to find out about relocating managerial authority and responsibility to lower levels in the organisation.

8 A recently appointed Purchasing Officer needs to learn what to look for when deciding which firms to buy goods from.

9 A chain that sells computer games would like ideas for improving the design and layout of its outlets.

10 The new Chief Executive of a major electronics manufacturer wants to see if his appointment is mentioned in the magazine.

Test 2

PART THREE

Questions 11–15

- Look at the graph below. It shows the average share prices of three companies – Grant International, HDC Union and the Lindel Group – over a nine-year period.
- Which year does each sentence (**11–15**) on the opposite page describe?
- For each sentence, mark one letter (**A–H**) on your Answer Sheet.
- Do not use any letter more than once.

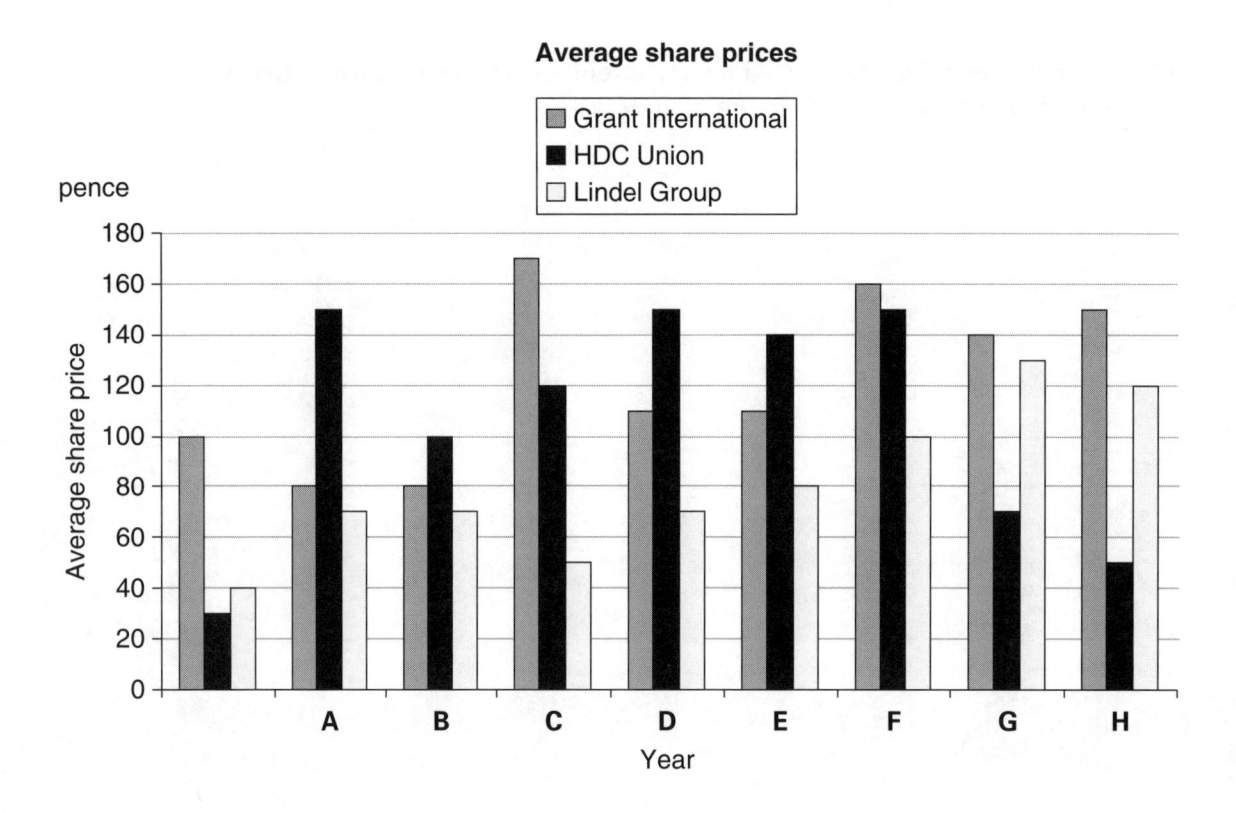

Average share prices

11 Although the share price for HDC Union rose and that of Grant International peaked, the share price of the Lindel Group experienced a decline.

12 While the share price for Grant International fell, those for HDC Union and the Lindel Group increased by approximately the same amount.

13 Although HDC Union's share price decreased in value, Grant International's remained steady and the Lindel Group continued its recovery.

14 Grant International's share price experienced an upturn, while the share price for both HDC Union and the Lindel Group declined.

15 HDC Union equalled previous highs in its share price, and Grant International and the Lindel Group also demonstrated an increase.

PART FOUR

Questions 16–22

- Read the article below about an insurance company.
- Are sentences **16–22** on the opposite page 'Right' or 'Wrong'? If there is not enough information to answer 'Right' or 'Wrong', choose 'Doesn't say'.
- For each sentence (**16–22**), mark one letter (**A, B** or **C**) on your Answer Sheet.

GOOD NEWS FROM AN INSURANCE COMPANY

For the fifth year in a row, the Loyalty Insurance Company has cut the cost of its house insurance. More than a million people with homes insured by the company will benefit from decreases of between two and four per cent on the amount they will have to pay this year. This move goes against the market trend, with other insurers increasing rates by an average one per cent.

'The level of claims has been lower than usual over this period, allowing us to make these welcome reductions,' says Malcolm Broad, Loyalty's General Manager.

Although the cost of insuring a car with Loyalty has increased by six per cent this year, it is still the smallest rise in the insurance industry; most other companies' rates are, on average, ten per cent higher than they were last year.

'The company has always believed in passing on any improvement in its financial position to its customers,' says Mr Broad. 'Without doubt, this has led to a continual expansion of our business over the past few years.'

Reading

16 This is the first year that Loyalty customers are paying less for their house insurance.

    A Right   **B** Wrong   **C** Doesn't say

17 Insuring a house with Loyalty will be at least four per cent cheaper than last year.

    A Right   **B** Wrong   **C** Doesn't say

18 Loyalty is performing in a different way from other insurance companies.

    A Right   **B** Wrong   **C** Doesn't say

19 This year, Loyalty has had the lowest number of claims ever recorded.

    A Right   **B** Wrong   **C** Doesn't say

20 Loyalty's car insurance is currently the cheapest available.

    A Right   **B** Wrong   **C** Doesn't say

21 It is Loyalty's policy to share its success with its customers.

    A Right   **B** Wrong   **C** Doesn't say

22 Malcolm Broad says that Loyalty's business started to grow last year.

    A Right   **B** Wrong   **C** Doesn't say

Test 2

PART FIVE

Questions 23–28

- Read the article below about a service which helps companies in difficulties.
- For each question (**23–28**) on the opposite page, choose the correct answer.
- Mark one letter (**A**, **B** or **C**) on your Answer Sheet.

THE INDEPENDENT EXECUTIVE SERVICE

How troubled businesses can benefit from the skills and experience of independent directors

Need a chairman in a hurry? An emergency finance director to sort out your cashflow problems? A leading venture capital company has set up a service which provides companies with temporary executives to help them out with particular tasks or periods of development. Michael Mann helped establish the Independent Executive Service (IES) in the late eighties and, as Director of the company, has led its expansion into markets at home and abroad.

The idea is simple. The skills that make a good businessperson who can launch a new business are quite different from those needed to run a medium-sized, mature operation. They are certainly not the skills needed if the business gets into difficulties, as can easily happen with fast-growing companies. It is in situations like this that the IES steps in.

It recruits people who have spent their careers in management, usually entrepreneurs themselves who have built up their own businesses and then sold them. The prospect of spending a limited time in a wide range of businesses is attractive to them. They want to do more in business, but don't want to go through the start-up process themselves again. As Mann explains, 'Most have experience of running their own companies and sorting out problems associated with a high-growth phase – this work comes naturally to them.'

'After preliminary discussions with the client company's HR Manager, we introduce five or six candidates to their Board of Directors. They then select the IES executive who best fits their requirements,' says Mann. 'We provide independent directors to many troubled companies, including those that we have already provided venture capital for. The service is free to these existing clients. For a fee, we also help out other companies which we think have a good recovery potential. Additionally, we have a great deal of repeat business from satisfied customers who buy our services again to help with a later stage of expansion.'

According to Mann, the first step for independent executives is often to establish how a business is meant to be run. 'In many small businesses, it is often unclear to Board members who is responsible for what in the company. Another common starting point is helping the existing management avoid bankruptcy. Only then is it possible to turn to more long-term issues.'

23 What service does the IES provide?

    A It hires out short-term directors to companies.
    B It advises companies on the recruitment of new directors.
    C It gives directors independent guidance on setting up new companies.

24 What is the idea on which the IES is based?

    A Different market sectors require different kinds of business skills.
    B Even skilled businesspeople need help in situations new to them.
    C Specialised leadership skills are needed to achieve fast growth.

25 Why do many IES executives like working for companies for limited periods?

    A They are intending to start up other companies in the future.
    B They are running their own companies at the same time.
    C They like the variety of working in many different companies.

26 Who makes the final decision about which executive will join a particular company?

    A the IES executive
    B the HR Manager
    C the Board of Directors

27 The IES offers its services without charge to companies it

    A has already invested in.
    B has previously provided directors for.
    C believes have a good chance of recovery.

28 IES executives often work with directors who are

    A unsure of their exact roles within their companies.
    B unclear about the causes of their companies' difficulties.
    C unaware that their companies are close to bankruptcy.

Test 2

PART SIX

Questions 29–40

- Read the introduction below to a business reference book.
- Choose the correct word to fill each gap from **A**, **B** or **C** on the opposite page.
- For each question (**29–40**), mark one letter (**A, B** or **C**) on your Answer Sheet.

Quick answers to key business questions

The information contained in this business reference book is directly useful to you and your business. **(29)** .... there is a lot of statistical material currently available, it tends to be about **(30)** .... industry or group of industries in particular. **(31)** .... is not terribly helpful to know what is **(32)** .... on in the pet-food industry if you **(33)** .... a chain of travel agencies. And knowing **(34)** .... businesses in the UK spend on training in total tells you very **(35)** .... about your own training budget.

The information provided in the book is based entirely on British data, and is relevant to businesses throughout the UK. Companies abroad do **(36)** .... things very differently, and if overseas research information were built into the data, this could **(37)** .... in inaccuracies in the figures.

This book will **(38)** .... you with business data that is useful for all types of businesses, **(39)** .... it will apply to you whichever business you are **(40)** .... It starts with the questions you might be expected to ask and then tries to answer them.

56

29	A	Although	B	Despite	C	Unless
30	A	the	B	one	C	every
31	A	There	B	It	C	This
32	A	getting	B	taking	C	going
33	A	keep	B	run	C	work
34	A	how	B	whose	C	what
35	A	little	B	few	C	less
36	A	other	B	any	C	some
37	A	result	B	lead	C	cause
38	A	produce	B	offer	C	supply
39	A	but	B	so	C	whereas
40	A	in	B	for	C	at

Test 2

PART SEVEN

Questions 41–45

- Read the two emails below.
- Complete the form on the opposite page.
- Write a word or phrase (in CAPITAL LETTERS) or a number on lines **41–45** on your Answer Sheet.

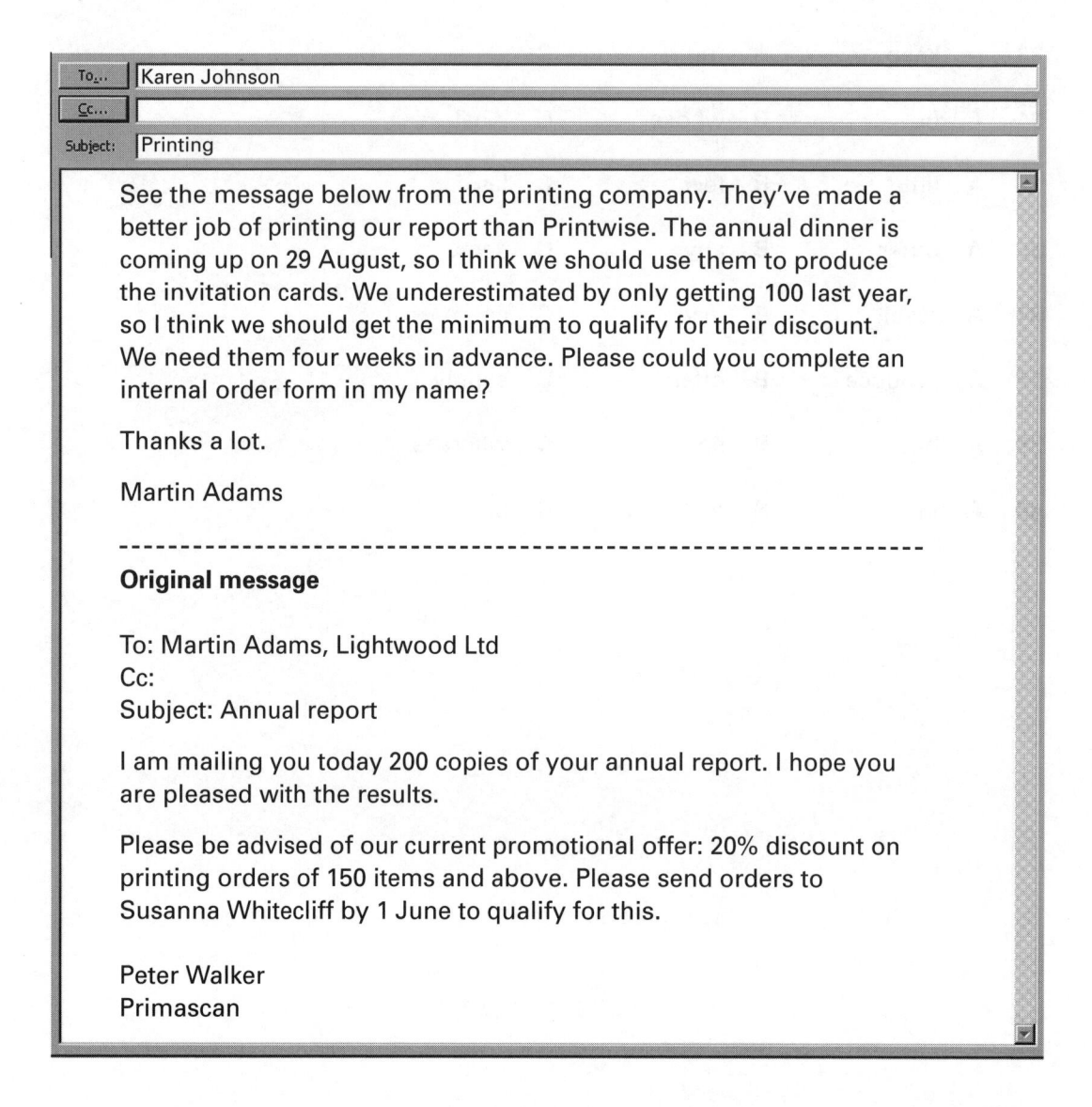

To...: Karen Johnson
Cc...:
Subject: Printing

See the message below from the printing company. They've made a better job of printing our report than Printwise. The annual dinner is coming up on 29 August, so I think we should use them to produce the invitation cards. We underestimated by only getting 100 last year, so I think we should get the minimum to qualify for their discount. We need them four weeks in advance. Please could you complete an internal order form in my name?

Thanks a lot.

Martin Adams

Original message

To: Martin Adams, Lightwood Ltd
Cc:
Subject: Annual report

I am mailing you today 200 copies of your annual report. I hope you are pleased with the results.

Please be advised of our current promotional offer: 20% discount on printing orders of 150 items and above. Please send orders to Susanna Whitecliff by 1 June to qualify for this.

Peter Walker
Primascan

Lightwood Ltd

Printing Order Form

Name of printing company: (41) ....

Type of document: (42) ....

Date required: (43) 1st 2009

Quantity required: (44) ....

Requested by (full name): (45) ....

Test 2

WRITING

PART ONE

Question 46

- You have just received a message that a new client, Jorge Ruiz, is arriving at your office tomorrow afternoon at 2 o'clock.
- Write a **memo** to your secretary, Helen Jones:
  - telling her about Mr Ruiz's visit
  - explaining why you might be late
  - telling Helen what to do with Mr Ruiz until you arrive.
- Write **30–40** words on your Answer Sheet.

MEMO

To: Helen Jones
From:
Date: 1/6/08
Subject: Visit of Jorge Ruiz

PART TWO

Question 47

- Read part of a letter below from Susan Dalton, the Sales Manager of a company that produces screens for computers.

> My company produces screens which fit in front of computer monitors and protect computer operators' eyes in strong or tiring lighting conditions. These screens are new on the market, but we have fully tested them. The trade price is $50 per screen.
>
> We would be glad to send a representative to demonstrate our product on your premises. I am confident that your staff will notice a great improvement in comfort.

- Write a **letter** to Ms Dalton:
  - explaining what your company does
  - saying why your company is interested in the product
  - enquiring about the possibility of a discount
  - suggesting a date for a demonstration.
- Write **60–80** words on your Answer Sheet.
- Do not include any postal addresses.

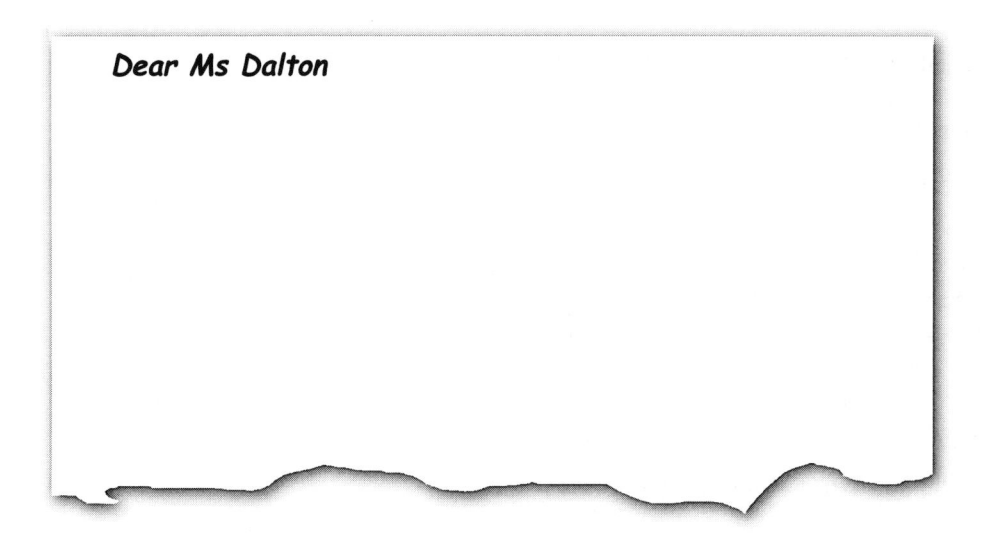

Dear Ms Dalton

Test 2

LISTENING Approximately 40 minutes (including 10 minutes' transfer time)

PART ONE

Questions 1–8

- For questions **1–8**, you will hear eight short recordings.
- For each question, mark **one** letter (**A**, **B** or **C**) for the correct answer.

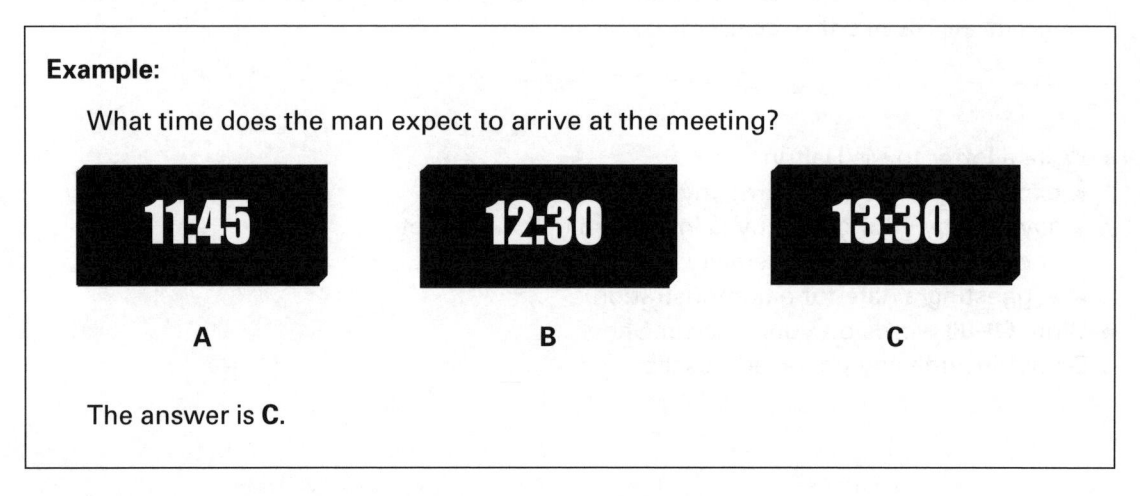

Example:

What time does the man expect to arrive at the meeting?

11:45	12:30	13:30
A	B	C

The answer is **C**.

- After you have listened once, replay each recording.

1 Which graph is the man talking about?

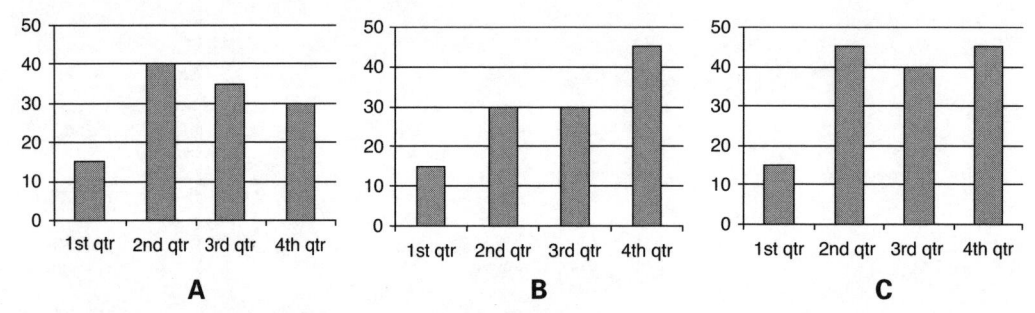

A   B   C

2 Which jobs will be created when the company relocates?

  A customer service advisers
  B packing assistants
  C delivery drivers

Listening

3 Why are the brochures late?

   A staff illness
   B faulty vehicles
   C broken machinery

4 What will Mediband's new owners do?

   A employ fewer staff
   B relocate the company
   C expand production

5 When will the sales conference be held?

6 Which chart shows exports of mobile phones this year?

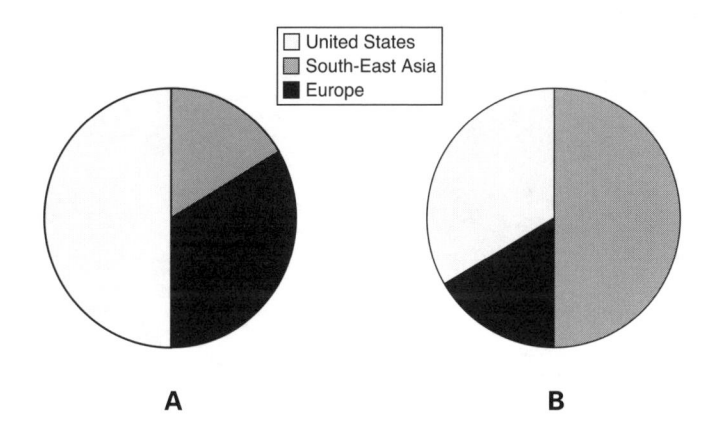

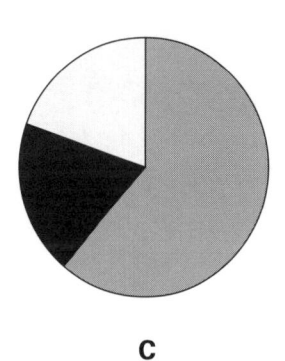

Test 2

7 Which day is the meeting arranged for?

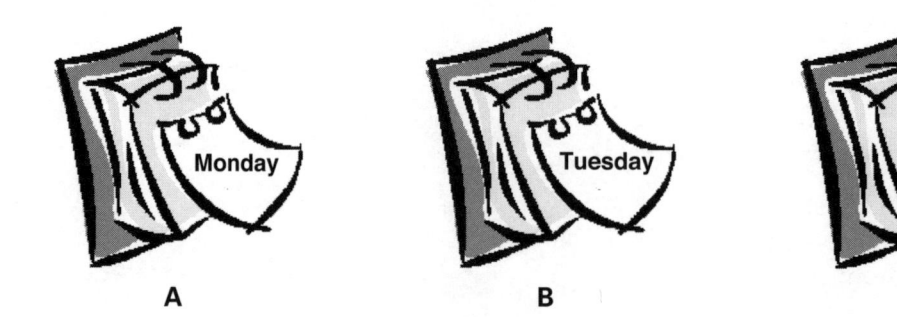

A. Monday
B. Tuesday
C. Wednesday

8 Why is the man phoning the suppliers?

    A   to report a problem
    B   to order a part
    C   to request information

PART TWO

Questions 9–15

- Look at the notes below.
- Some information is missing.
- You will hear a man giving some information about gifts to order for staff who have performed well.
- For each question (**9–15**), fill in the missing information in the numbered space using **a word**, **numbers** or **letters**.
- After you have listened once, replay the recording.

NOTES		
Website:	(9)	www. .... .co.uk
Order:		
15 x silver calculators at	(10)	£ .... *each*
5 x leather picture holders at		*£42 each*
Size:	(11)	.... *by 30 cm*
1 x £95	(12)	.... *Gift Desk Set*
Mark's mobile:	(13)	*07950* ....
Call him before	(14)	.... *tomorrow*
Order must be here by	(15)	.... *April*

Test 2

PART THREE

Questions 16–22

- Look at the notes below about a marketing conference.
- Some information is missing.
- You will hear part of a report to colleagues about the marketing conference.
- For each question (**16–22**), fill in the missing information in the numbered space using **one** or **two** words.
- After you have listened once, replay the recording.

NOTES ON MARKETING CONFERENCE

Subject of most useful presentation: **(16)** ....

Name of presenter: **(17)** Susan ....

Most important part of conference: **(18)** making ....

Harry Baxter wants to order **(19)** ....

Bentley High-Tech

    City where headquarters are located: **(20)** ....

    Representative plans to visit us in **(21)** ....

    Representative particularly wants to find out about **(22)** ....

PART FOUR

Questions 23–30

- You will hear a radio interview with a successful businessman called Nigel Player, who runs an airline on the island of Alderney.
- For each question (**23–30**), mark **one** letter (**A**, **B** or **C**) for the correct answer.
- After you have listened once, replay the recording.

23 Where was Nigel Player's first job?

    A   at a transport company
    B   at a bank
    C   at an electronics firm

24 Nigel Player left his successful career because he wanted to

    A   retire from the business world.
    B   start a new business.
    C   write a business book.

25 Nigel Player decided to open a food shop in Alderney because

    A   he found the food shops there unsatisfactory.
    B   there were not many food shops there.
    C   he was able to buy an existing shop quite cheaply.

26 Why wasn't Nigel Player satisfied with the existing airline?

    A   It charged him too much.
    B   It was unreliable during the holiday season.
    C   It only operated in the summer.

27 Nigel Player felt bringing food to Alderney by boat would be too

    A   expensive.
    B   difficult in bad weather.
    C   slow.

28 Nigel Player decided to run a passenger airline service because

    A   his supermarket customers persuaded him to.
    B   the other airline only operated twice a week.
    C   it seemed more profitable than his retail business.

Test 2

29 What most helped Nigel Player run a passenger airline?

    A having friends already in the business
    B understanding the financial background
    C knowing about flying freight

30 What does Nigel Player say is the secret of his company's success?

    A its commitment to customer service
    B its commitment to expansion
    C its commitment to employing local people

You now have 10 minutes to transfer your answers to your Answer Sheet.

Speaking

SPEAKING   12 minutes

SAMPLE SPEAKING TASKS

PART ONE

In this part, the interlocutor asks questions to each of the candidates in turn. You have to give information about yourself and express personal opinions.

PART TWO

In this part of the test, you are asked to give a short talk on a business topic. You have to choose one of the topics from the two below and then talk for about one minute. You have one minute to prepare your ideas.

A: **What is important when . . . ?**

Selecting a speaker for a business seminar

- Experience of speaker
- Specialist topics
- Fees

B: **What is important when . . . ?**

Arranging a social event for business clients

- Venue
- Food and drink
- Cost of event

69

Test 2

PART THREE

In this part of the test, the examiner reads out a scenario and gives you some prompt material in the form of pictures or words. You have 30 seconds to look at the task prompt, an example of which is below, and then about two minutes to discuss the scenario with your partner. After that, the examiner will ask you more questions related to the topic.

For **two** or **three** candidates

Scenario

> I'm going to describe a situation.
>
> **The large company you work for is moving to a new site and is planning facilities for its staff. Talk together for about two minutes* about some of the facilities the company could have for staff and decide which three would be best.**
>
> Here are some ideas to help you.

* three minutes for groups of three candidates

Prompt material

Facilities for Staff

- Car park
- Personal lockers
- Canteen
- Social activity room
- Sports area
- Library

Follow-on questions

- Is there any other facility which a big company should provide? (Why?/Why not?)
- Should small companies also provide staff facilities? (Why?/Why not?)
- Do employees work better if they have good facilities? (Why?/Why not?)
- Do you think staff should pay to use any of the facilities? (Why?/Why not?)
- Are there any disadvantages for companies in providing staff facilities? (Why?/Why not?)

Test 3

READING AND WRITING   1 hour 30 minutes

READING

PART ONE

Questions 1–5

- Look at questions **1–5**.
- In each question, which sentence is correct?
- For each question, mark one letter (**A**, **B** or **C**) on your Answer Sheet.

Example: 0

Telephone message

Claudia Lang caught 9.30 flight – due here 11.30 now, not 12.30.

When does Claudia Lang expect to arrive?

A   9.30
B   11.30
C   12.30

The correct answer is **B**, so mark your Answer Sheet like this:

| 0 | A | B | C |

1

> **Goods will be despatched to you on receipt of payment in full.**

A   You must pay the whole amount before goods are sent.
B   You needn't pay in full until your goods arrive.
C   Your goods will be sent when you have paid a deposit.

2

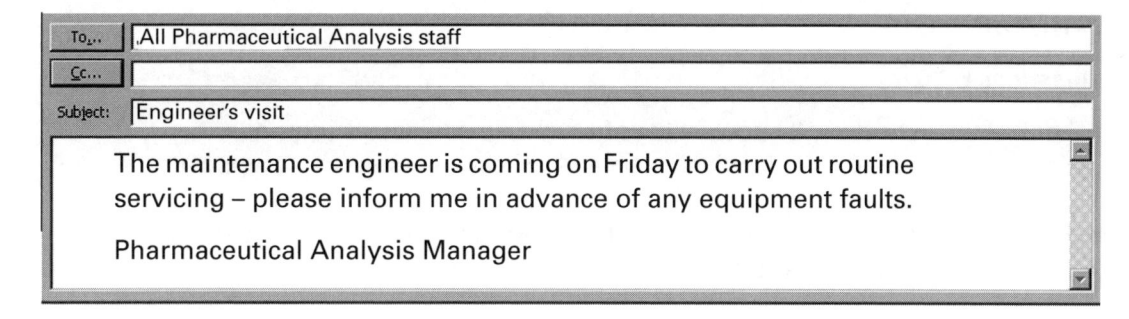

To...	All Pharmaceutical Analysis staff
Cc...	
Subject:	Engineer's visit

The maintenance engineer is coming on Friday to carry out routine servicing – please inform me in advance of any equipment faults.

Pharmaceutical Analysis Manager

- **A** The engineer was called because of a problem with equipment.
- **B** Staff should tell the engineer about any equipment problems they have found.
- **C** The manager wants to know before Friday about problems with equipment.

3

Creasey's Office Support
A broad range of small business services provided by a workforce with combined experience of over 45 years.
Tel: 01358 782323

- **A** Creasey's, a small company, wishes to become partners with a more experienced organisation.
- **B** Creasey's is combining with other small businesses to provide a variety of office services.
- **C** Creasey's offers the services of its skilled personnel to small companies.

4

Maria,
Enclosed is the schedule for this year's training days.
If you can't manage any of them, contact John.

What should Maria do?

- **A** Notify John of the training days she might miss.
- **B** Inform John about the schedule for his training days.
- **C** Ask John how to arrange her training schedule.

5

DFN Motors to extend its Michigan assembly plant next year – 600 new jobs
Recruitment and training to start January
CLICK HERE FOR FULL STORY

- **A** A car company is increasing the capacity of its factory in Michigan.
- **B** The staff at a car factory in Michigan will increase to 600 people.
- **C** A car factory in Michigan is training recruits to start work in January.

Test 3

PART TWO

Questions 6–10

- Look at the list below. It shows a list of articles in a business journal.
- For questions **6–10**, decide which article (**A–H**) each person on the opposite page should read.
- For each question, mark the correct letter (**A–H**) on your Answer Sheet.
- Do not use any letter more than once.

CONTENTS

A	Bank charges on currency exchange: are you getting the best deal?
B	Career ladder: executive employment opportunities
C	Branding: re-inventing your product
D	Setting up staff retirement schemes
E	Which policy can best protect your premises against damage or theft?
F	Getting out of the red: reducing overheads
G	Transport issues – how they affect your business
H	Exporting your brand – how to achieve this

6   Mesut Akman runs a successful cycle-manufacturing business and wants to sell some established product lines to overseas markets.

7   Lena Feldt needs to pay off debts and cut costs at the executive employment agency where she is a senior manager.

8   Janice Carter, PA to the Chief Executive at Central Bank, is looking for an insurance deal to cover company property.

9   Michael Kaminski wants to organise pensions for part-time employees in the advertising company where he is Head of Human Resources.

10 Nicolas Perez, owner of an insurance company, wants to change his company's image to attract more customers in the domestic market.

Test 3

PART THREE

Questions 11–15

- Look at the chart below. It shows a manufacturing company's expenditure on recruitment and training, and its production levels over a ten-year period.
- Which year does each sentence (**11–15**) describe?
- For each sentence, mark one letter (**A–H**) on your Answer Sheet.
- Do not use any letter more than once.

Expenditure on recruitment and training, and numbers of units produced

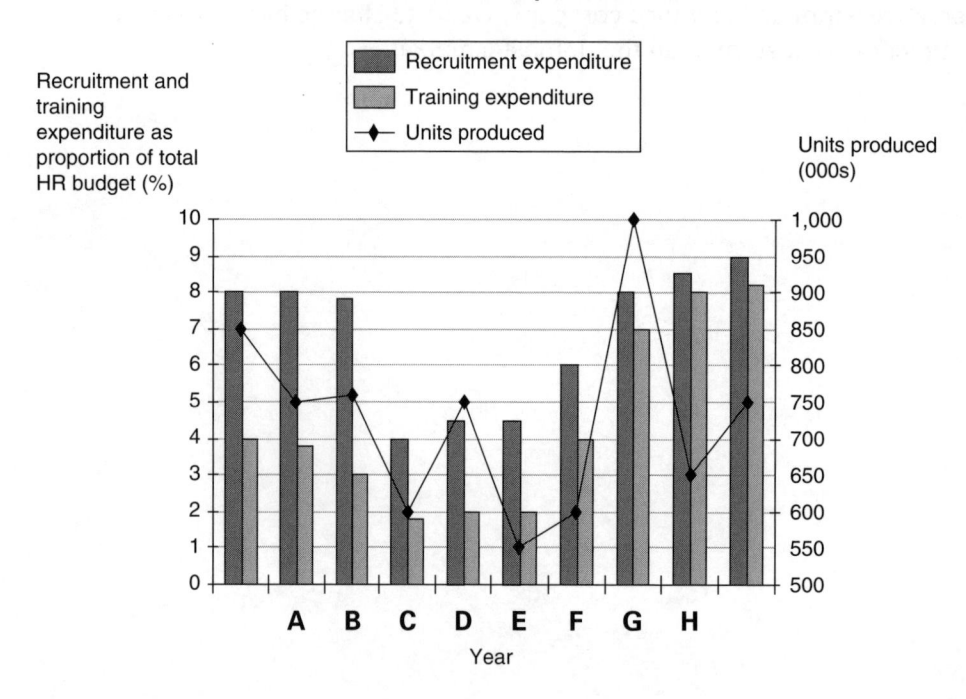

11 A drop in expenditure on both recruitment and training resulted in a decline in the number of units produced.

12 Production dropped sharply this year, even though the training budget saw an increase on the previous year.

13 Despite the fact that spending on recruitment and training increased only slightly, output experienced a significant upturn.

14 Fewer units were produced than the previous year, even though levels of recruitment spending were maintained, and the training budget was only slightly cut.

15 In this year, the amount spent on training went up again, and production rose more steeply than at any other time during the period.

PART FOUR

Questions 16–22

- Read the report below about a talk on Customer Relationship Marketing (CRM).
- Are sentences **16–22** on the opposite page 'Right' or 'Wrong'? If there is not enough information to answer 'Right' or 'Wrong', choose 'Doesn't say'.
- For each sentence (**16–22**), mark one letter (**A, B** or **C**) on your Answer Sheet.

CRM – Marketing in the 21st century

With over 1,000 published newspaper articles, three successful books and his current job as Chairman of his own marketing consultancy, Swan Partners, Richard Swan is well qualified to lecture on marketing. At the industry's recent annual conference, he focused his talk on Customer Relationship Marketing (CRM).

According to Swan, existing customers are between three and eight times more likely to buy than a non-customer with the same profile, so increasing customer loyalty is important: if you record the measurements of someone's jeans, next time you can offer them a pair that fit exactly; note which hotel guests ask for ice in their drinks and produce it next time they visit. Although it is essential for effective CRM to record customer information on a good computer database, the real skill is in interpreting what your customers tell you and knowing what promises they *think* you have made.

Swan believes that success requires an equal mix of market research, delivering what the customer expects, finding any weak areas in the system and asking customers for their after-sales opinions and suggestions. 'But,' he warns, 'approach CRM with care. If you can't measure customer response, then it's better to keep to more traditional marketing methods.'

Reading

16 In addition to being an author, Richard Swan is actively involved in the business world.

    A Right   **B** Wrong   **C** Doesn't say

17 Swan Partners are the market leaders in delivering CRM.

    A Right   **B** Wrong   **C** Doesn't say

18 One aspect of Swan's talk was to explain the advantages of developing a solid customer base.

    A Right   **B** Wrong   **C** Doesn't say

19 Swan believes the CRM approach is best suited to service industries.

    A Right   **B** Wrong   **C** Doesn't say

20 Having the right technology is the most important component of successful CRM.

    A Right   **B** Wrong   **C** Doesn't say

21 In Swan's opinion, achieving company growth depends on a combination of several factors.

    A Right   **B** Wrong   **C** Doesn't say

22 Swan thinks all companies should move from old-fashioned marketing to CRM.

    A Right   **B** Wrong   **C** Doesn't say

PART FIVE

Questions 23–28

- Read the article below about the qualities of a good boss.
- For each question (23–28) on the opposite page, choose the correct answer.
- Mark one letter (**A**, **B** or **C**) on your Answer Sheet.

What makes a good boss better?

Different businesses require different management skills. But some of these skills are common to all good managers. Everyone's opinion of what makes a good boss differs. Each work environment places different demands on managers, and a good boss in one workplace might not be as effective elsewhere.

In large companies, where delegation and organisation are important, the role of the boss or chief executive is to encourage and generally get the best out of his or her managers. In a small business, however, the boss's job is to ensure, without the help of any middle management, that staff at all levels meet targets. This requires a different set of skills.

'Being a good manager is important in any organisation, but it's particularly so in small businesses,' says David Harvey, Director of management-research company Optima. 'This is because in a small company, the Director shapes the company culture and the overall atmosphere in the workplace. Without effective leadership, the company will fail, regardless of the strengths or weaknesses of the competition.'

The most successful small businesses are those where the boss can get the employees to take an active role in the development of the organisation. It isn't just about paying staff more. A sense of purpose is also important. This doesn't have to take the form of ambitious mission statements, which are so popular with some management schools. Instead, it's about communicating a set of business priorities that everyone in the organisation feels is important and that they want to achieve. If you take a holiday company, this sense of purpose can be about focusing on first-class customer service, so that all holidaymakers feel well looked-after on arrival in a resort.

A good boss cares about the development of staff and recognises that the company will also gain if staff are encouraged to achieve their potential and succeed in their careers. People development depends on appropriate training and providing the right environment in which people can learn, either formally or on the job.

It is possible to acquire leadership skills. While some people have an instinctive understanding of what makes a good manager, others can learn as they go along.

Reading

23 What does the writer say about good managers in the first paragraph?

   A They would succeed in all types of organisation.
   B They share certain qualities with one another.
   C They learn their skills in a good working environment.

24 What does the writer say the CEO of a large company must do?

   A Encourage staff at all levels.
   B Set higher performance targets.
   C Motivate managers to achieve what they can.

25 Why does David Harvey believe directors are important in small companies?

   A They are responsible for staying ahead of competitors.
   B No one else takes part in the decision-making.
   C Their style directly affects all the staff.

26 According to the writer, what can a boss do to promote success in a small company?

   A Give staff the opportunity to earn a good salary.
   B Make sure staff share the same aims.
   C Follow the advice of management schools.

27 Why does the writer mention the holiday company?

   A to suggest a different approach to motivating staff
   B to show the importance of providing good service to customers
   C to give an example of some possible business values in practice

28 According to the writer, why is staff development important for a company?

   A Staff work better if their individual careers are supported.
   B Staff need to keep up to date with developments in the industry.
   C Staff with problems can be helped to deal with them.

PART SIX

Questions 29–40

- Read the report below about the growth of low-cost airlines.
- Choose the correct word to fill each gap from **A**, **B** or **C** on the opposite page.
- For each question (**29–40**), mark one letter (**A**, **B** or **C**) on your Answer Sheet.

LOW-COST AIR TRAVEL

For most organisations, it is very important to reduce travel costs. That is (29) .... more and more companies are booking flights with low-cost airlines; in fact, this (30) .... of the market has grown dramatically in recent years.

Low-cost airlines offer tickets at well below the prices (31) .... by ordinary airlines, but (32) .... still meet the same safety standards and regulations. Operating costs are reduced in a number of (33) .... Firstly, customers book directly with the airline, either on the internet or (34) .... the telephone. Low-cost airlines do not, (35) .... , have to pay commission to travel agents. Further savings are (36) .... , as these airlines do not issue tickets – they simply give customers a reference number. Passengers do not normally receive postal confirmation of their booking (37) .... they ask for it, which some do in order to carry proof (38) .... booking. Finally, low-cost airlines do not usually offer (39) .... in-flight services.

(40) .... low-cost airlines may soon become normal practice in the business world.

82

Reading

29	A	what	B	when	C	why
30	A	branch	B	sector	C	department
31	A	charged	B	cost	C	paid
32	A	must	B	shall	C	ought
33	A	methods	B	ways	C	approaches
34	A	through	B	along	C	over
35	A	however	B	indeed	C	therefore
36	A	made	B	had	C	done
37	A	if	B	unless	C	as
38	A	at	B	for	C	of
39	A	much	B	many	C	more
40	A	Choose	B	Choosing	C	Chosen

Test 3

PART SEVEN

Questions 41–45

- Read the memos below.
- Complete the conference booking form on the opposite page.
- Write a word or phrase (in CAPITAL LETTERS) or a number on lines **41–45** on your Answer Sheet.

HARRIS & GALWAY LTD

MEMO

To: Tony Moss
From: Olivia Granger
Date: 10 May
Subject: Conference booking

Please let me have details of the conference you're organising, as I need to book a venue asap. Last year, the event was held in the Red Room at the Grand Hotel. Are you planning to use the same hotel again? If not, you could try the Regal Hotel. The food is excellent, and rooms are available between 3 and 9 August. Are you invoicing the Marketing Department for this?

HARRIS & GALWAY LTD

MEMO

To: Olivia Granger, Marketing
From: Dan Ottoman, Sales
Date: 11 May
Subject: Conference booking

Tony is not in the office this week and he has asked me to tell you that the dates have changed from 3–5 August to 7–9 August. He's not planning to use the Grand – the hot meals and the service there were terrible. He is going to use your suggestion – he's heard it's a good hotel. He'd like to book a buffet lunch. Our department is paying for the event this year.

84

HARRIS & GALWAY LTD
CONFERENCE BOOKING FORM

Conference organiser (full name): (41) ....

Venue requested: (42) ....

Date(s) required: (43) ....

Catering requirements: (44) ....

Department to invoice: (45) ....

Test 3

WRITING

PART ONE

Question 46

- Your company has decided to make a change to its working hours.
- Write an **email** to staff in your department:
  - describing the change to working hours
  - explaining the reason for this change
  - saying when the working hours will change.
- Write **30–40** words on your Answer Sheet.

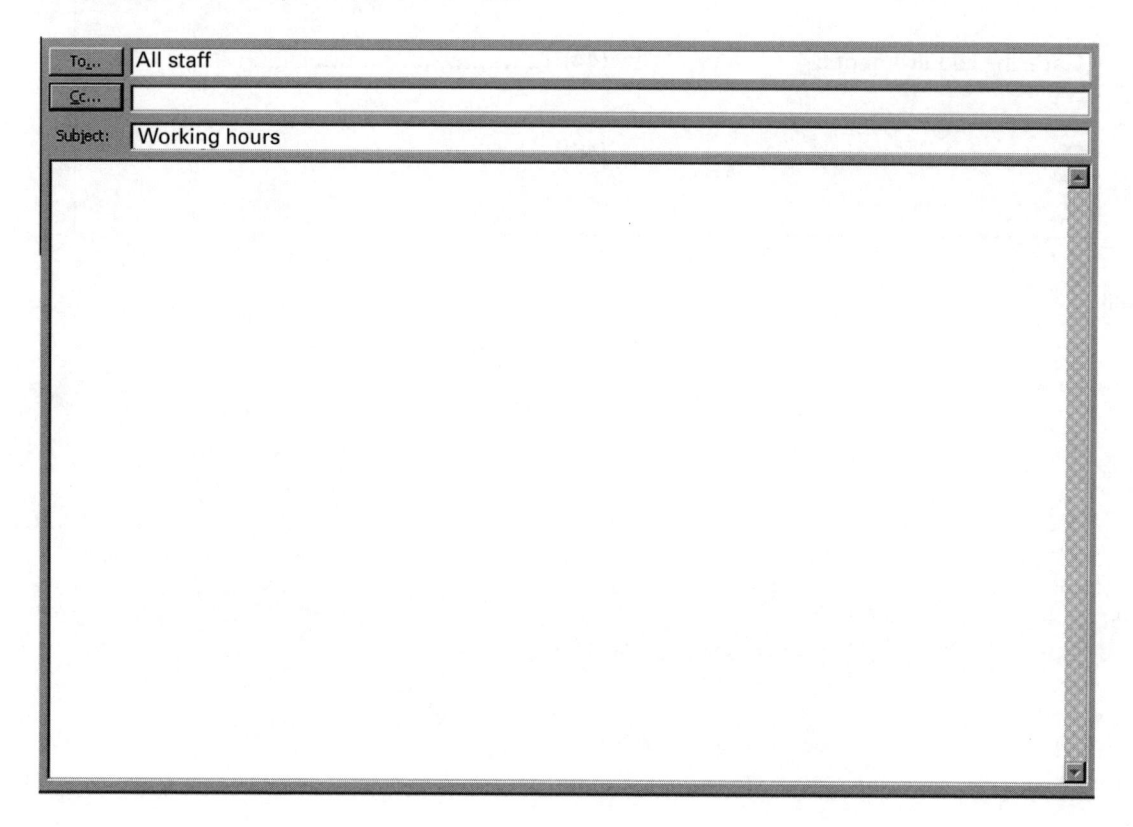

To:...	All staff
Cc...	
Subject:	Working hours

PART TWO

Question 47

- Read part of a letter below from Peter Morgan, the Marketing Manager of Speedex, a delivery company.

> I'm writing to tell you about an exciting new service that we at Speedex are offering in your area. We are a small distribution company and can guarantee to deliver anywhere within the local area for the cheapest price currently available. If you are interested in our service, please contact me for further details.

- Write a **letter** to Peter Morgan:
  - acknowledging his letter
  - saying why you need a new delivery company
  - explaining what type of goods you need delivering
  - inviting him to visit you at your office.
- Write **60–80** words on your Answer Sheet.
- Do not include any postal addresses.

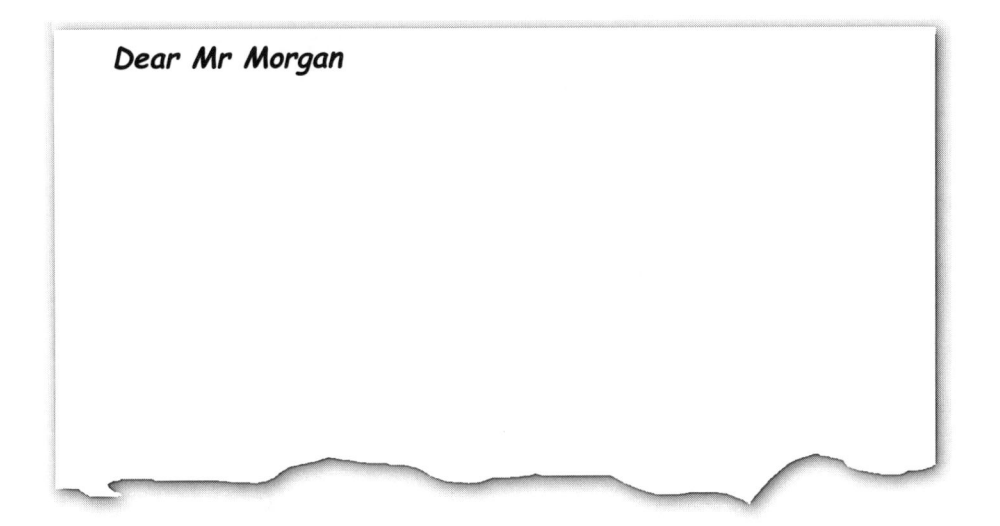

Dear Mr Morgan

Test 3

LISTENING   Approximately 40 minutes (including 10 minutes' transfer time)

PART ONE

Questions 1–8

- For questions **1–8**, you will hear eight short recordings.
- For each question, mark **one** letter (**A**, **B** or **C**) for the correct answer.

> **Example:**
>
> Who is Anna going to write to?
>
> **A** the staff
> **B** the supplier
> **C** the clients
>
> The answer is **A**.

- After you have listened once, replay each recording.

1   When will the next meeting be?

    A   23rd March
    B   24th March
    C   25th March

2   Which of the goods were delivered?

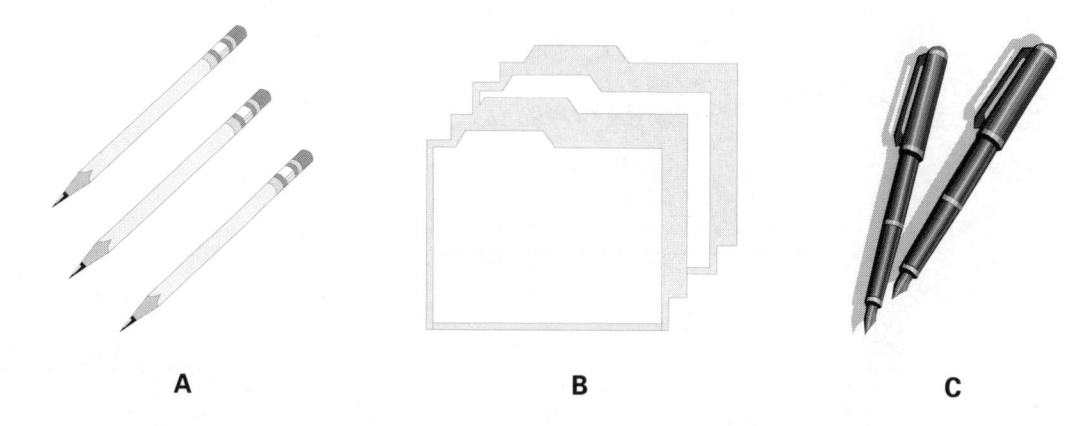

    A   B   C

88

3 Why is the man apologising?

   A   because he's late
   B   because he's made a mistake
   C   because he's lost something important

4 What is the cover of the new brochure like?

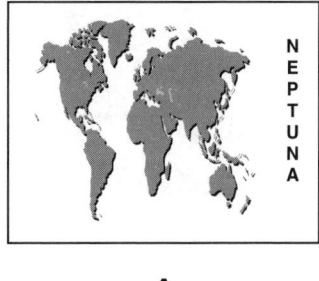

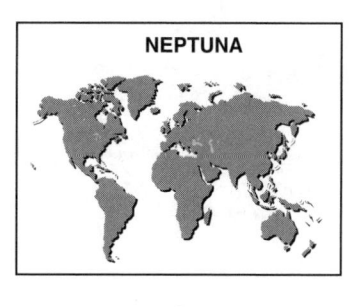

   A   B   C

5 Which chart is correct?

   Number of hours lost to staff illness

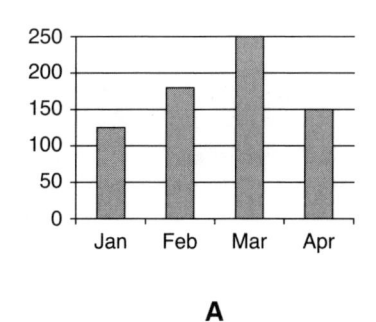

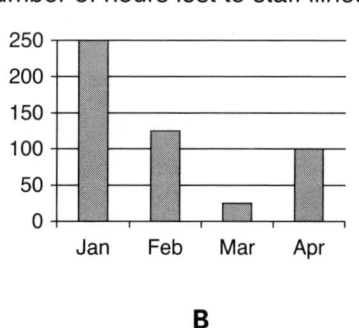

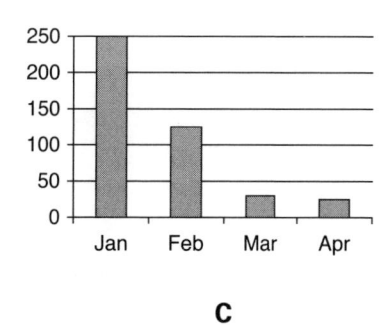

   A   B   C

6 What are staff still forgetting to do with company cars?

   A   record the distance travelled
   B   refill them with petrol
   C   tidy them inside

7 What do the speakers say about Esther Wong?

   A   She resigned.
   B   She was promoted.
   C   She retired.

Test 3

8 Which chart is the speaker talking about?

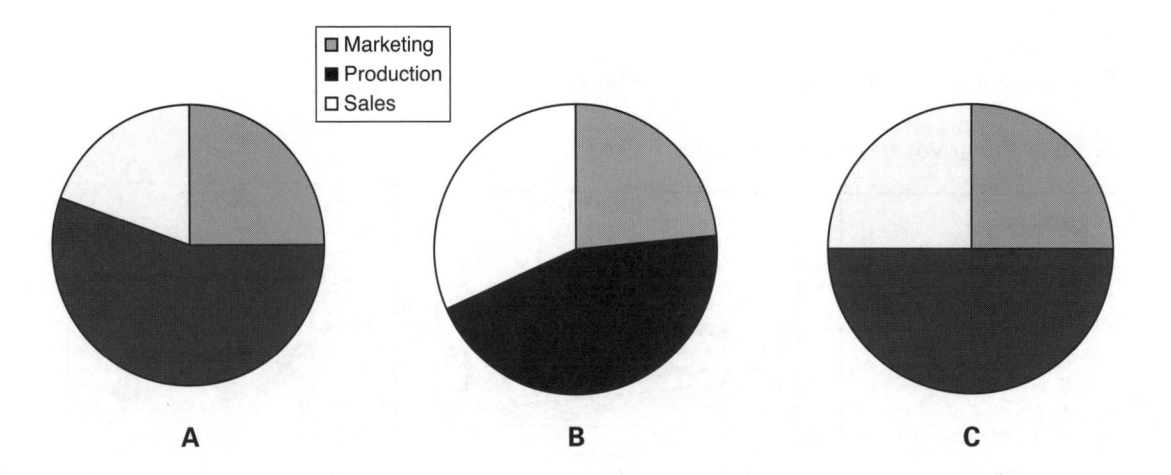

☐ Marketing
■ Production
☐ Sales

A   B   C

Listening

PART TWO

Questions 9–15

- Look at the notes below.
- Some information is missing.
- You will hear a journalist talking to the Head of Public Relations of a large supermarket chain.
- For each question (**9–15**), fill in the missing information in the numbered space using **a word**, **numbers** or **letters**.
- After you have listened once, replay the recording.

Notes for article

COMPANY: Rezzo

CHIEF EXECUTIVE: (9) Jane ....

CURRENT POSITION

Pre-tax profits to September:	(10) £ .... million
Current share price:	(11) .... pence
Increase in sales per square metre:	(12) .... %
Reduced prices on a total of	(13) .... product lines

FUTURE PLANS

Will build	two new hypermarket stores
Size of each new hypermarket:	(14) .... square metres
Total amount of space for non-food goods will be	(15) .... %

91

PART THREE

Questions 16–22

- Look at the notes below.
- Some information is missing.
- You will hear a man giving a talk about his work and career.
- For each question (**16–22**), fill in the missing information in the numbered space using **one** or **two** words.
- After you have listened once, replay the recording.

NOTES ON TALK

Name of speaker:	Patrick Greene
First business of his own:	(16) a .... company
Name of present company:	(17) ....
The company runs public-speaking courses aimed at	(18) ....
Titles of two main courses:	(19) 'Giving ....'
	(20) '................................'
Courses begin with • Voice work	
• How to use a	(21) ....
Last part of course • Handling	(22) ....
• Timing a talk	

Listening

PART FOUR

Questions 23–30

- You will hear an interview between a radio presenter and a businessman, Tim Black, about British people relocating and going to work outside the UK.
- For each question (**23–30**), mark one letter (**A**, **B** or **C**) for the correct answer.
- After you have listened once, replay the recording.

23 In Tim Black's company, which people usually get relocated abroad?

    A   those who have previous experience of working abroad
    B   those who have specific skills to offer
    C   those who are more senior

24 What reason does Tim give for companies sending fewer employees abroad?

    A   There aren't enough suitable candidates.
    B   Companies are less willing to fund it.
    C   Working abroad is no longer seen as leading to promotion.

25 According to Tim, what is the current trend amongst British workers?

    A   Commuting long distances is less common.
    B   Working in London is their first choice.
    C   Living in the countryside has grown in popularity.

26 What financial advice does Tim give employees thinking of relocating abroad?

    A   Buy extra health insurance.
    B   Ensure that pension fund payments will still be made.
    C   Ask your company to rent out your house.

27 What was Tim's company doing in Dubai?

    A   manufacturing building materials
    B   designing a public building
    C   constructing an office building

28 What did Tim's company arrange before he left?

    A   a short visit to Dubai before moving there
    B   a personal contact with the team in Dubai
    C   a language course in Arabic

29 What arrangements did Tim make for accommodation?

    A He bought an expensive house.
    B He stayed in a company flat.
    C He arranged to move in with a colleague.

30 Tim expected to stay in Dubai for some time because he was

    A going to supervise a lengthy project.
    B starting a new area of work.
    C aiming to get lots of experience.

You now have 10 minutes to transfer your answers to your Answer Sheet.

SPEAKING   12 minutes

SAMPLE SPEAKING TASKS

PART ONE

In this part, the interlocutor asks questions to each of the candidates in turn. You have to give information about yourself and express personal opinions.

PART TWO

In this part of the test, you are asked to give a short talk on a business topic. You have to choose one of the topics from the two below and then talk for about one minute. You have one minute to prepare your ideas.

> **A: What is important when . . . ?**
>
> Using a travel agent for booking business trips
>
> - Experience of staff
> - Range of services
> - Hours of business

> **B: What is important when . . . ?**
>
> Running business meetings
>
> - Agenda
> - Chairperson
> - Taking notes

Test 3

PART THREE

In this part of the test, the examiner reads out a scenario and gives you some prompt material in the form of pictures or words. You have 30 seconds to look at the task prompt, an example of which is below, and then about two minutes to discuss the scenario with your partner. After that, the examiner will ask you more questions related to the topic.

For **two** or **three** candidates

Scenario

> I'm going to describe a situation.
>
> **A large company is organising a three-day conference for its employees from different parts of the country. Talk together for about two minutes* about the things that need to be organised and decide which three are the most important.**
>
> Here are some ideas to help you.

* three minutes for groups of three candidates

Prompt material

- Location and venue
- Transport
- Accommodation
- Catering
- Speakers
- Equipment for speakers
- Displays
- Evening entertainment

Speaking

Follow-on questions

- How would you inform people about the conference?
- Why are conferences important for companies?
- Why is it important for business people to attend conferences?
- What facilities should conference centres provide? (Why?)
- What would you like a conference to be about? (Why?)
- What kind of conference would you like to go to? (Why?)

Test 4

READING AND WRITING   1 hour 30 minutes

READING

PART ONE

Questions 1–5

- Look at questions **1–5**.
- In each question, which sentence is correct?
- For each question, mark one letter (**A**, **B** or **C**) on your Answer Sheet.

Example: 0

Telephone message

Claudia Lang caught 9.30 flight – due here 11.30 now, not 12.30.

When does Claudia Lang expect to arrive?

A   9.30
B   11.30
C   12.30

The correct answer is **B**, so mark your Answer Sheet like this:

| 0 | A | **B** | C |

1

MEMO

To: Factory staff
From: Factory Manager
Date: 19 November 2008
Subject: Quality control

The new system starts Monday week. Please read attached leaflet and contact me if there are any queries.

What does the Factory Manager want the staff to do?

A   suggest additions to quality-control instructions
B   ask if they don't understand something
C   contact him when the new system starts

98

2

> **Notice to retailers**
> Owing to production delays and unexpected demand, we regret that product No. AS/524B is out of stock.

- A This product is currently unavailable.
- B Manufacture of this product is discontinued.
- C The suppliers have temporarily withdrawn this product.

3

> The seminar is from 4.30 to 6.00, with time allowed for questions from the audience.
>
> Refreshments are served at 6.00.

- A The speaker will respond to questions if time allows.
- B There will be time to ask questions during the seminar.
- C It will save time if questions are left until refreshments are served.

4

> **VP50 PROJECTOR**
> Details of retailers available on
> www.viewpoint.projectors.com
> To arrange demonstration, ring your nearest stockist.

- A Customers can purchase a VP50 projector from a sales outlet online.
- B Customers can view how the VP50 projector works on their PC.
- C Customers can use the internet to see where VP50 projectors are sold.

5

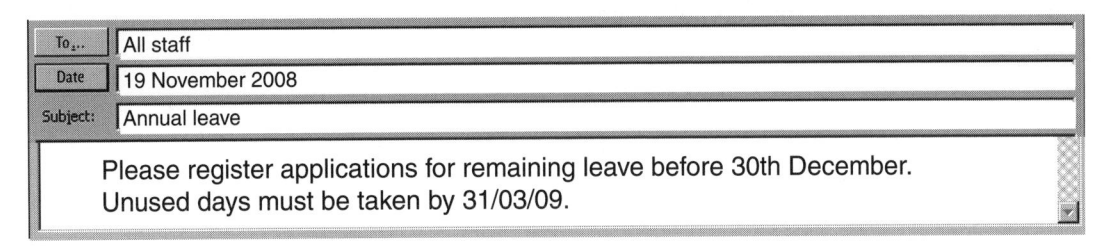

> To: All staff
> Date: 19 November 2008
> Subject: Annual leave
>
> Please register applications for remaining leave before 30th December. Unused days must be taken by 31/03/09.

- A The company cancels any unused annual holiday at the end of the year.
- B The company will not allow any more holidays until next year.
- C The company needs to know about employees' holiday plans.

PART TWO

Questions 6–10

- Look at the leaflet below. It shows a list of talks organised by a marketing association for its members.
- For questions **6–10**, decide which event (**A–H**) is the most suitable for each person on the opposite page to attend.
- For each question, mark one letter (**A–H**) on your Answer Sheet.
- Do not use any letter more than once.

CM Marketing Association
Events for March

A Business-to-business marketing: secrets of successful networking

B Improving e-marketing performance

C Using market researchers – why and how?

D IT in presentations – what's available and how to use it

E Advertising, PR or marketing: which is king?

F Making the appearance of products more attractive

G Well-trained staff – an important marketing tool

H Tripton Motors, marketing success story

6 Wolfgang Kuhlmann's director wants him to attend a talk on the benefits of updating employees' marketing skills.

7 The Product Manager of Smiths Engineering wants to know about the effectiveness of computer graphics when giving talks to major clients.

8 Barbara Gorska's company advertises mainly through magazines, but she needs to make more effective use of the company's website.

9 An advertising trainee has read a research report on the importance of design and packaging and would like more information.

10 Computer services provider Martin McDonald wants to find out about ways of making useful contacts in other companies.

Test 4

PART THREE

Questions 11–15

- Look at the charts below. They show a publishing company's sales in eight countries over the same four-month period in 2006 and 2007.
- Which chart does each sentence (**11–15**) on the opposite page describe?
- For each sentence, mark one letter (**A–H**) on your Answer Sheet.
- Do not use any letter more than once.

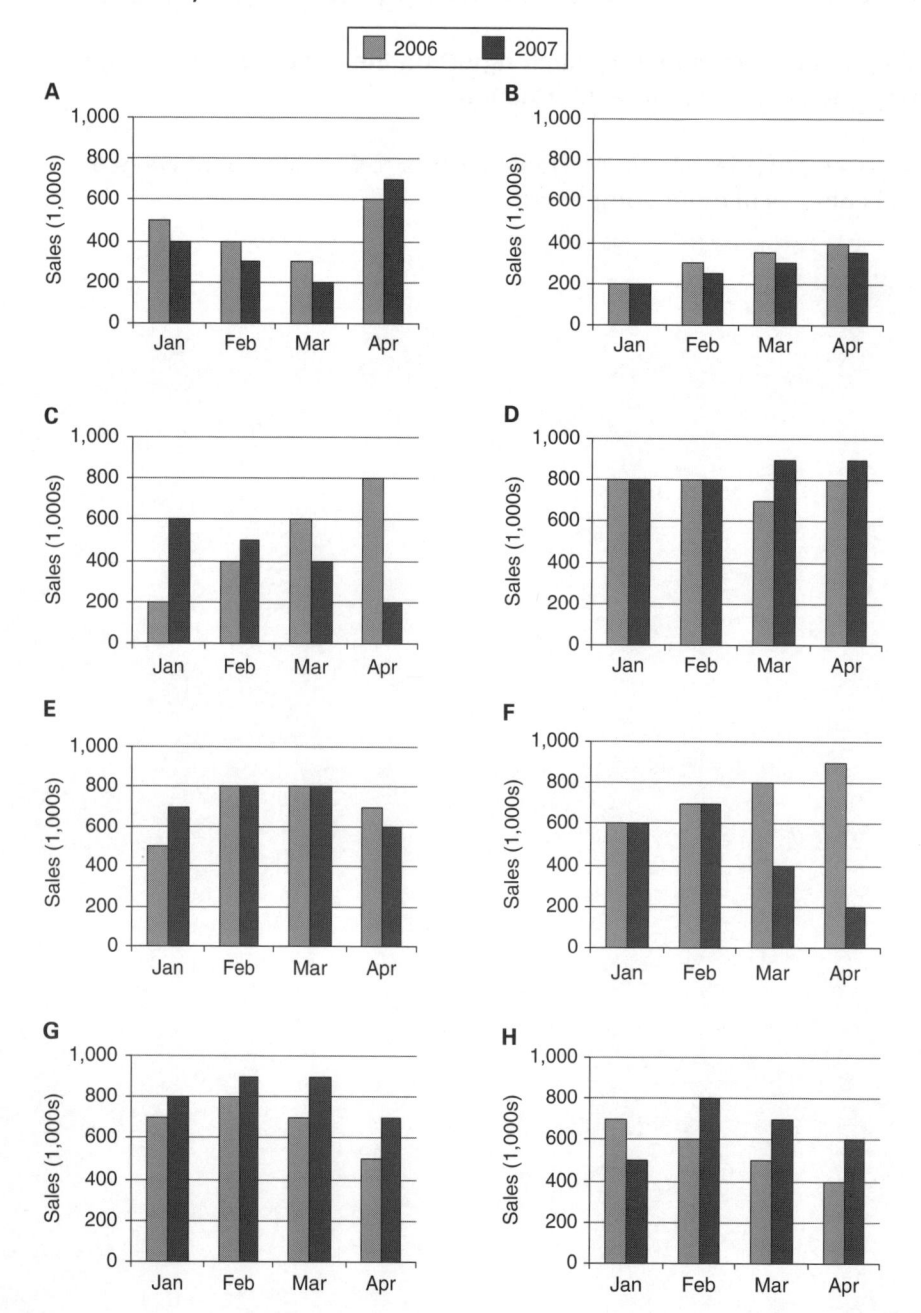

11 In the first year, sales rose steadily, but in the next, they started to fall after the middle of the period.

12 In both years, declining sales were followed by a dramatic recovery in the fourth month.

13 Although sales rose at first in both years, they ended the period below their opening levels.

14 The first year saw sales climb steadily during the period, while in the second, they declined throughout.

15 Although sales at the beginning of the period were the same in both years, overall performance was better in the second year.

PART FOUR

Questions 16–22

- Read the article below about a supermarket chain in the UK.
- Are sentences **16–22** on the opposite page 'Right' or 'Wrong'? If there is not enough information to answer 'Right' or 'Wrong', choose 'Doesn't say'.
- For each sentence (**16–22**), mark one letter (**A**, **B** or **C**) on your Answer Sheet.

Reducing a supermarket chain's costs

A few years ago, the Sainsbury's supermarket chain asked management consultancy Cobalt to find ways of significantly reducing its operating costs and increasing the turnover in its stores.

The team, at first made up of four Cobalt project managers and five Sainsbury's colleagues, was challenged to make £300m of savings within five years. Beginning with a pilot exercise which cut the cost to the company of own-brand olive oil by £400,000, the team looked at a number of products and found potential savings in many areas, including stock reduction and distribution changes.

To motivate the team, whenever a saving was recorded on a board in the centre of Cobalt's open-plan office, everyone clapped the team achievement.

As the project progressed, it expanded, with Cobalt recruiting and training extra team members to look at more products at the same time.

After just over a year, the team began training Sainsbury's 130 trading managers and buyers in its recommended approach. With savings now over £100m, Sainsbury's was so pleased that it decided to expand the approach to the whole of its operations.

Cobalt is now driving a team of 50 Sainsbury's colleagues towards a new target: corporate savings of £700m.

16 Sainsbury's contracted Cobalt with the aim of improving profitability.

    A Right   **B** Wrong   **C** Doesn't say

17 The team consisted entirely of Cobalt staff.

    A Right   **B** Wrong   **C** Doesn't say

18 The price of olive oil was reduced for customers.

    A Right   **B** Wrong   **C** Doesn't say

19 Cobalt contacted Sainsbury's whenever a saving was recorded.

    A Right   **B** Wrong   **C** Doesn't say

20 The number of people involved in the project increased.

    A Right   **B** Wrong   **C** Doesn't say

21 The project included training Sainsbury's staff.

    A Right   **B** Wrong   **C** Doesn't say

22 The project has now come to an end.

    A Right   **B** Wrong   **C** Doesn't say

PART FIVE

Questions 23–28

- Read the article below from a company's staff magazine, about a recent training course.
- For each question (**23–28**) on the opposite page, choose the correct answer.
- Mark one letter (**A**, **B** or **C**) on your Answer Sheet.

Training for new sales staff

Our pipe systems division has just held a successful two-day training course for new sales staff from all over the world.

This course was rather different from usual. Our products, like those of our competitors, are well known in our main markets, and our aim now is to introduce those products into other countries. This course was targeted at the new sales staff employed to carry out that strategy, and who therefore needed to be prepared to face strong competition.

Unlike our other training events, this course was held in the factory, despite our careful plans to ensure that the improvements to the training centre were finished in time, and that regular courses were moved somewhere else. But at almost the last moment, it became clear that numbers attending the course were too great for everyone to fit in. And so the factory it was.

Following presentations on our products and production processes, there were practical workshops, in which participants could watch each other trying to sell to possible customers. These ended with what proved to be the most popular section of the training – an in-depth discussion of the difficulties of selling.

Also included in the programme was a tour of the factory, where special attention was given to our efforts to achieve high quality. We were particularly pleased to show that we are committed to high environmental standards. What was perhaps rather unexpected for many participants was how much we ourselves use the pipe systems we produce: for drinking water, cooling, and so on.

There wasn't time to cover every aspect of selling, but participants learned how different methods can suit different people. More importantly, the training meant our staff from around the world could meet and learn from each other. While the two presentations – by senior managers from Head Office – provided information, it was the contact with colleagues that created this feeling of belonging.

The participants' questionnaires showed they enjoyed being in the factory. However, this cannot be the regular venue, because of the problems it would cause for production. There was great interest in meeting again for a higher-level course, and we plan to hold one next autumn. And there seems to be no reason to change the balance of the programme between presentations and workshops.

And now – go out and sell!

23 The training course was held because the division

  A plans to launch a new range of products.
  B intends to expand into new markets.
  C needs to compare its products with those of competitors.

24 Why was it impossible to use the training centre?

  A It was too small for the number of participants.
  B It was in use for another training course.
  C It was having work done to it.

25 Why did the participants like the workshops most?

  A They had the chance to talk about how to do their job.
  B They were able to practise selling.
  C They learned a great deal about the products.

26 What surprised some participants during the tour of the factory?

  A the company's success in its efforts to protect the environment
  B the care which the company takes to check product quality
  C the number of ways in which the company uses its own products

27 The writer thinks the most valuable aspect of the training for staff was

  A the opportunity to meet senior managers.
  B the chance to learn the same sales methods.
  C the opportunity it provided for team-building.

28 What is the result of the questionnaires?

  A Future courses will be held in the factory.
  B The participants will be offered another course.
  C The balance of the course will be changed.

PART SIX

Questions 29–40

- Read the text below about a sports retailer.
- Choose the correct word to fill each gap from **A**, **B** or **C** on the opposite page.
- For each question (**29–40**), mark one letter (**A**, **B** or **C**) on your Answer Sheet.

Alstar Sport

Alstar Sport is a leading sports retailer in the United Kingdom. The company was **(29)** .... in 1971 by the owner of a small leisure centre in Leeds. After **(30)** .... steadily from a company with just a few stores to **(31)** .... with over 120, Alstar Sport was finally floated **(32)** .... the London Stock Exchange in 1995. The company's principal aim **(33)** .... it was first founded has been to **(34)** .... its customers with high-quality sports and leisure products **(35)** .... competitive prices.

The company's main customers regularly participate in sport, **(36)** .... the stores also attract people who are **(37)** .... looking for leisure and casual wear.

Alstar Sport is still based in Leeds, where the company's head office is located. The company has recently **(38)** .... the sports group Eddie Wilkins plc. According to Peter Carmichael, the Chief Executive, this **(39)** .... provide an excellent opportunity for growth and expansion in the United Kingdom. 'It's given us a **(40)** .... larger market than we've had until now,' he says.

29	A	introduced	B	presented	C	established
30	A	grew	B	grown	C	growing
31	A	one	B	it	C	this
32	A	in	B	on	C	for
33	A	when	B	during	C	since
34	A	equip	B	supply	C	serve
35	A	by	B	to	C	at
36	A	if	B	although	C	whereas
37	A	simply	B	quite	C	hardly
38	A	achieved	B	acquired	C	added
39	A	would	B	need	C	should
40	A	much	B	very	C	such

Test 4

PART SEVEN

Questions 41–45

- Read the two memos below.
- Complete the request form for tickets for the business fair on the opposite page.
- Write a word or phrase (in CAPITAL LETTERS) or a number on lines **41–45** on your Answer Sheet.

HOWLETT AND PINCHER

MEMO

To: Peter Hobbs
From: Maria Garcia
Subject: OnView Business Fair
Date: 17/11/08

I'm filling in the form for next year's Fair (Monday 10th to Saturday 15th July). I spoke to Jack Watson, Marketing Manager, who was planning to attend and was interested in the seminar on Effective Promotions, but he is no longer able to go. He thought the new Finance Manager was going instead. Can you confirm this and also let me know if there are any special requests such as accommodation?

HOWLETT AND PINCHER

MEMO

To: Maria Garcia
From: Peter Hobbs
Subject: OnView Business Fair
Date: 18/11/08

Jack was right – Andrea Harlock is now going to the Fair, but for the Tuesday only. She wants to go to the seminar on Funding Growth, so could you note that on the form? She will need a parking space, but accommodation isn't necessary, as she will return on the same day.

110

OnView Business Fair
Ticket request form

Company: *Howlett and Pincher*

Full name of person attending: **(41)** ....

Job title: **(42)** ....

Date(s) attending: **(43)** *2009*

Title of seminar(s) to be attended: **(44)** ....

Special requests: **(45)** ....

Test 4

WRITING

PART ONE

Question 46

- A new colleague, Marina Walker, has emailed you to ask for your help with writing a report on the German car market, but you cannot help her at the moment.
- Write an **email** to Marina:
  - explaining why you cannot help her
  - suggesting the name of another person
  - saying what relevant experience that person has.
- Write **30–40** words on your Answer Sheet.

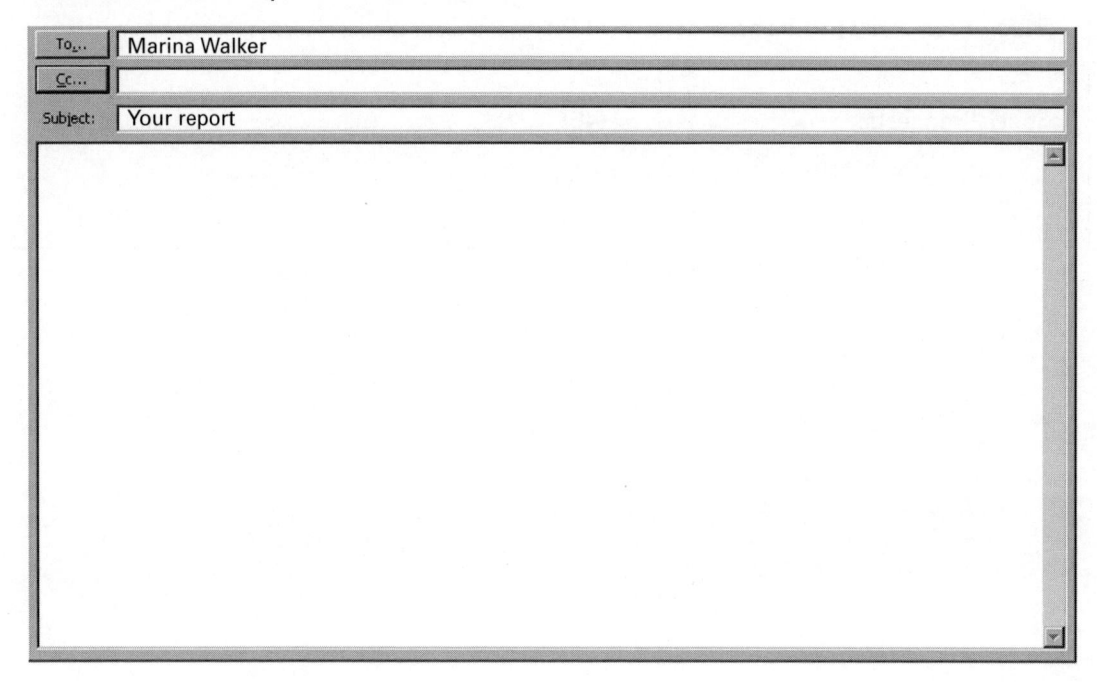

To:	Marina Walker
Cc:	
Subject:	Your report

PART TWO

Question 47

- Read part of a letter below from Joanne Kranz, who is the Production Manager in a factory near Athens which you are going to visit soon.

> With regard to your visit 5–6 December, please send me the details of your flight so that I can meet you at the airport and accompany you to our factory.
>
> At the moment, I am organising your programme. Please let me know if there is anything that you would particularly like to see or do in the factory.

- Write a **fax** to Ms Kranz:
    - thanking her for her letter
    - giving her your flight details
    - explaining what you would like to do in the factory
    - requesting hotel accommodation.
- Write **60–80** words on your Answer Sheet.
- Do not include any postal addresses.

Dear Ms Kranz,

Test 4

LISTENING   Approximately 40 minutes (including 10 minutes' transfer time)

PART ONE

Questions 1–8

- For questions **1–8**, you will hear eight short recordings.
- For each question, mark **one** letter (**A**, **B** or **C**) for the correct answer.

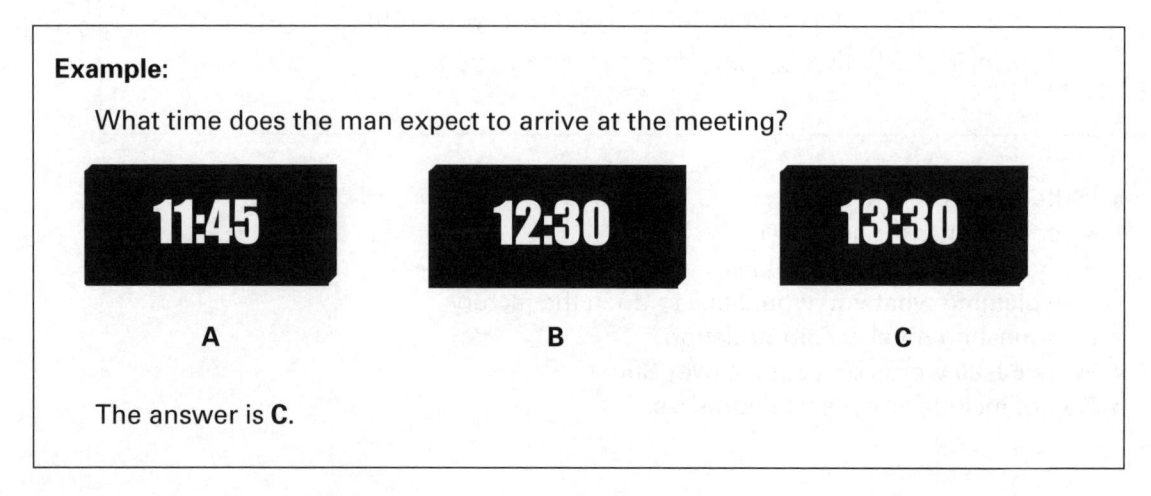

Example:

What time does the man expect to arrive at the meeting?

11:45	12:30	13:30
A	B	C

The answer is **C**.

- After you have listened once, replay each recording.

1   How many people attended the annual general meeting this year?

   A   about 100
   B   about 180
   C   about 250

2   Where will the man go first?

   A   the Presentation Room
   B   the Security Office
   C   the Production Department

114

Listening

3 Which brand is the market leader?

Sodex   *Thomsen*   LANDOR

    A   B   C

4 What time will the woman get to Oxford?

    A   9.45
    B   10.30
    C   10.45

5 Where will the woman find the file?

    A    B    C

6 Which chart shows the sales of sports clothing this month?

Total sales   Sports clothing

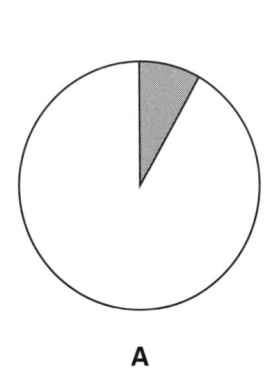

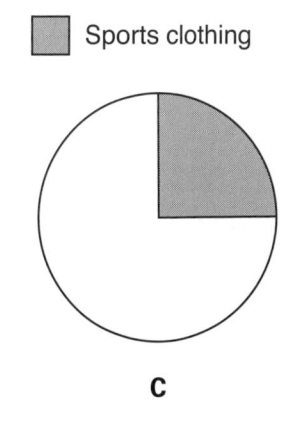

    A 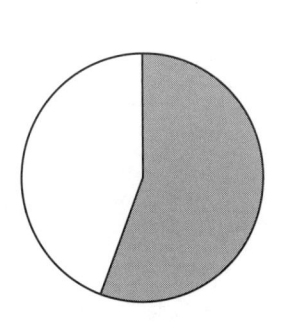   B   C

Test 4

7 Which department will get the biggest budget next year?

    A Sales
    B Production
    C Distribution

8 Which graph shows orders correctly?

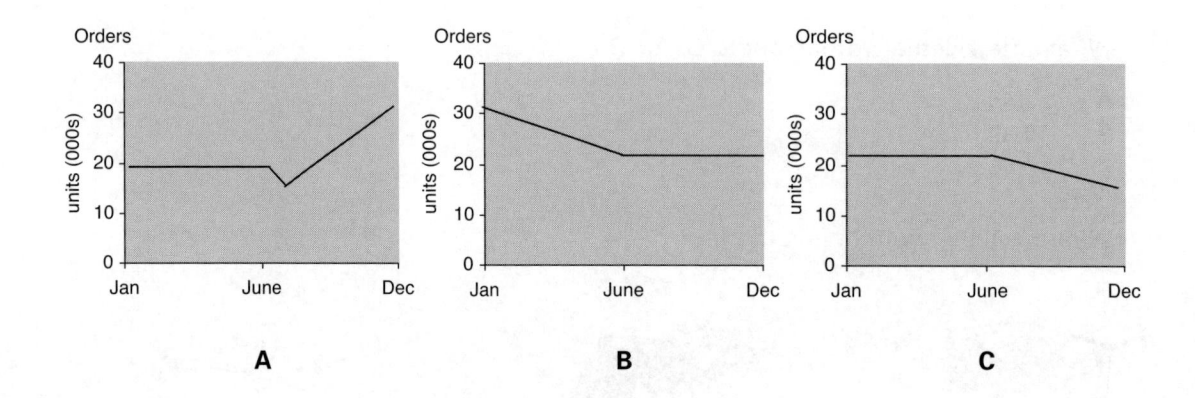

Listening

PART TWO

Questions 9–15

- Look at the notes below.
- Some information is missing.
- You will hear a man making an enquiry about ordering a new printer.
- For each question (**9–15**), fill in the missing information in the numbered space using **a word**, **numbers** or **letters**.
- After you have listened once, replay the recording.

CIT Computers – Customer Enquiry

Company name:	Davies and Baker
Contact name:	(9) James ....
Equipment required:	printer

SPECIAL REQUIREMENTS

Maximum width:	(10) .... cm
Print quality required:	(11) .... dots per cm
Speed required:	(12) .... pages per minute
Model number:	(13) ....
Agreed price:	(14) £ ....
Delivery date:	(15) Friday ....

Test 4

PART THREE

Questions 16–22

- Look at the notes about one month's events in a city's business community.
- Some information is missing.
- You will hear part of a radio programme about business events.
- For each question (**16–22**), fill in the missing information in the numbered space using **one** or **two** words.
- After you have listened once, replay the recording.

BUSINESS EVENTS

Thursday June 12th and Friday June 13th

Name of conference:	(16)	'..'
Location:	(17)	....
Name of event:		
Day one:		'Financing Joint Ventures'
Day two:	(18)	'............................. Law'
Main speaker:	(19)	Dr James ....

Wednesday June 18th

Name of event:		'Fast Forward'
Location:		Ocean Park Hotel
Introduce new business people to	(20)	....

Friday June 27th

Name of seminar:	(21)	'..'
Location:		The City University
Speaker: Paul Miller	(22)	.... of Westwick Business School
For details, ring:		0202 06103

118

Listening

PART FOUR

Questions 23–30

- You will hear a discussion between Philip Michael, the Chief Executive of IKD, a design company, and a journalist from the business section of a national newspaper.
- For each question (**23–30**), mark **one** letter (**A**, **B** or **C**) for the correct answer.
- After you have listened once, replay the recording.

23 What do IKD's clients like about the company's location?

    A   It is easy to get to.
    B   It is in beautiful surroundings.
    C   It is hidden away.

24 How do IKD's designers work on their ideas?

    A   They use computers and solid models.
    B   They use computers alone.
    C   They use computers and pencil drawings.

25 Who is IKD's biggest client at the moment?

    A   a motorbike manufacturer
    B   a household goods manufacturer
    C   a car manufacturer

26 Who is IKD working with to improve their designs?

    A   their clients' R and D departments
    B   university staff
    C   freelance artists

27 What do companies value most about IKD?

    A   the quality of its designs
    B   its competitive fees
    C   the speed it works at

28 A bike designed by IKD recently

    A   received an award.
    B   appeared on the front of biking magazines.
    C   won a race.

Test 4

29 What happens to most of IKD's designs?

    A   They go straight into production.
    B   They are rejected before production.
    C   They are kept for future production.

30 IKD's customers pay by giving the company

    A   a single agreed fee per project.
    B   a fee related to sales.
    C   a fee per hour of designers' time.

You now have 10 minutes to transfer your answers to your Answer Sheet.

Speaking

SPEAKING   12 minutes

SAMPLE SPEAKING TASKS

PART ONE

In this part, the interlocutor asks questions to each of the candidates in turn. You have to give information about yourself and express personal opinions.

PART TWO

In this part of the test, you are asked to give a short talk on a business topic. You have to choose one of the topics from the two below and then talk for about one minute. You have one minute to prepare your ideas.

> A: What is important when . . . ?
>
> Choosing a computer skills course
>
> - Topics
> - Size of group
> - Qualification offered

> B: What is important when . . . ?
>
> Deciding the price of a product
>
> - Cost of production
> - Cost of similar products
> - Type of customer

Test 4

PART THREE

In this part of the test, the examiner reads out a scenario and gives you some prompt material in the form of pictures or words. You have 30 seconds to look at the task prompt, an example of which is below, and then about two minutes to discuss the scenario with your partner. After that, the examiner will ask you more questions related to the topic.

For **two** or **three** candidates

Scenario

> I'm going to describe a situation.
>
> **A supermarket chain is opening a new store. Talk together for about two minutes* about ways of promoting the store on the first day, and decide which way would be best.**
>
> Here are some ideas to help you.

* three minutes for groups of three candidates

Prompt material

- Offering special discounts
- Having a famous person open the store
- Giving away free gifts
- Holding a competition with prizes
- Having live music

Follow-on questions

- What kind of free gifts might the company offer? (Why?)
- What kind of competition might the company hold? (Why?)
- How would you advertise the opening? (Why?)
- Are shoppers influenced by one-day promotions? (Why/Why not?)
- Does the layout and appearance of a store influence you? (Why/Why not?)

KEY

Test 1 Reading

Part 1
1 C 2 A 3 B 4 A 5 A

Part 2
6 C 7 G 8 F 9 A 10 E

Part 3
11 E 12 D 13 B 14 H 15 F

Part 4
16 A 17 A 18 C 19 B 20 C
21 B 22 B

Part 5
23 B 24 A 25 B 26 C 27 B
28 C

Part 6
29 C 30 C 31 A 32 B 33 A
34 C 35 B 36 C 37 B 38 A
39 C 40 B

Part 7
41 THORPE COLLEGE
42 MAR(CH) THE 6(TH) / THE 6(TH) OF MAR(CH) / 6/3 / 3/6
43 16
44 (MR / MS / MRS / MISS) JAN PARTRIDGE
45 (THE) (MANAGEMENT) COURSE SECRETARY

Test 1 Writing

Part 1

Sample A

> To: Human Resources Manager
> Subject: Staffing problem
> Dear Sir/Madam,
> I am writing to you concerning staffing problem. Our department currently has a lot of work, you know it's about the party of New Year, but unluckly, our secretary's mother was ill, she must to take care of her, so she has take several weeks off. Could you arrang a temporary secretary for me. Thankyou!
> Yours sincerely

Band 5
This is a very good attempt at the task set. All the content points are achieved. It is not error-free, but no effort is required by the reader.

Sample B

> Dear Mr Elmiger
>
> We have a lot of work and many people are ill.
> We have not time for all the works.
> The secretary must away for the work.
> Can come 3 people from the secretary to us?
>
> Karin

Band 2
This is an inadequate attempt at the task set. Only the first content point is covered. No reason is given for the secretary's absence, and the third point is unclear.

Part 2

Sample C

> Dear Miss Foster
>
> I express an interest in your company's services. I describe my company's training needs, we are an established company providing a wide range of training services for all kinds of bussniss. we have our own purpose-built centre where we hold courses, or training can be offered at the client's own premises if preferred. we offer excellent value for money and a full 100% satisfaction guarantee. So please inviting you to a meeting next week.

Band 1
The first and fourth points are addressed, but the candidate's response is mostly lifted from the input and is largely irrelevant.

Sample D

> Dear Miss Foster,
>
> I write this letter for interesting in your company services, getting this informating from internet, we know you can offer venual for trainging.
>
> On 13 June we want to held a training new staff about our products, it will have 30 persons attend to the course.
>
> Due to your purpose-built centre is near to our company and have suitable place, we can work with together.
>
> I invite you come to my company next week.
>
> I look forward hearing from you.
>
> Linda

Band 3
The third point is not achieved. A number of errors are present, but overall this is a reasonable achievement of the task set.

Test 1 Listening

Part 1

1 B   2 C   3 C   4 C   5 A   6 C
7 C   8 A

Part 2

9 GILLMANN (INTERNATIONAL)
10 DT19055
11 131 (CM)
12 ZY88320
13 (£)162
14 (£)27
15 19(TH)

Part 3

16 EXHIBITION / (EXIBITION)
17 (WORKSHOP(S)) COMMUNICATION
18 (SIMPLY) LEADERSHIP
19 ACCOMMODATION / (ACCOMODATION)
20 FITNESS CENTRE / FITNESS CENTER
21 MOVING FORWARD
22 (ENQUIRY / INQUIRY) FORM(S)

Part 4

23 B   24 A   25 B   26 C   27 A
28 C   29 B   30 C

Tapescript

Listening Test 1

This is the Business English Certificate Preliminary 4, Listening Test 1.

Part One. Questions 1 to 8.

For questions 1–8, you will hear eight short recordings. For each question, mark one letter (A, B or C) for the correct answer.

Here is an example: Who is Emily going to write to?

[pause]

Man: Emily, that supplier we use has become very unreliable, and we've decided to look for another one.
Woman: Seems a good idea.
Man: We don't need to inform our clients, but could you send a note round to all our departments when we've decided who to replace the supplier with?
Woman: Yes, of course.

[pause]

The answer is A.

Now we are ready to start.

After you have listened once, replay each recording.

[pause]

One: What is the quotation for one thousand brochures with colour photos?

[pause]

Man: How much can you quote for our brochure order?
Woman: If you want the colour photos, it'll be more expensive. Er, for two thousand, it'll be two thousand five hundred pounds, or for a thousand, it'll be one thousand, five hundred pounds. Without colour photos, the price goes down a bit.
Man: How much?
Woman: Er, for a thousand, it would be one thousand two hundred.

[pause]

Two: When will the new Personnel Officer start work?

[pause]

Woman: Jane is leaving next week, isn't she?
Man: Yes. We recruited the new Personnel Officer in July, but because she has to relocate from

Key

Newcastle, I don't think she'll be able to begin until October.
Woman: Well, we'll need to arrange some temporary cover for September.
Man: OK. I'll look into it.

[pause]

Three: Which pie chart is correct?

[pause]

Man: . . . and I'm pleased to report that here at WTM, our market share has increased by ten per cent, taking us ahead of our rivals PTA for the first time. Of course, AVC are still the market leaders with a fifty-five-per-cent share, so . . .

[pause]

Four: Why is Jane unhappy about Michael's report?

[pause]

Woman: Where's the report I asked for, Michael?
Man: Sorry, Jane, it's here, just finished. It's a bit late, but . . .
Woman: That doesn't matter. Has anyone else seen it?
Man: I circulated copies internally. I thought you asked me to.
Woman: Not before I'd checked it first. If you've made mistakes in it, it won't be very good for the department.

[pause]

Five: What is the woman's current job with BGT?

[pause]

Man: Can you tell me about your work with BGT?
Woman: Well, I started in nineteen ninety-two as Account Manager. The General Manager was keen to promote young staff quickly, so shortly after that, I became Project Team Leader. My boss, the Project Manager, became General Manager last year.
Man: And you were promoted?
Woman: Yes, I took his place.

[pause]

Six: What does the speaker think the company should do?

[pause]

Man: So, what will you do to keep the business going through this difficult time?

Woman: As a low-cost airline, we're happy with the numbers using the internet to reserve tickets, and customers report that our prices are competitive. We now need to look at cutting back on in-flight catering, as sales of snacks have really dropped recently.

[pause]

Seven: What does the woman need to get?

[pause]

Man: Is there a sound system in the seminar room?
Woman: Well, we've got a microphone, and there's a video player there . . .
Man: Mmm, I'm not sure the MD will use it. A flipchart is essential, though.
Woman: Oh, I never thought of that, I'll fetch one now. Shall I remove the video?
Man: No, leave it, I might use it in the afternoon.

[pause]

Eight: Which graph shows the company figures?

[pause]

Man: Figures published today by the Falmouth Group received a mixed reaction. Although production costs increased at a slower rate during the second half of the year, profits continued to fall.

[pause]

That is the end of Part One.

[pause]

Part Two. Questions 9 to 15.

Look at the notes below.

Some information is missing.

You will hear a man discussing an order from an office supply company.

For each question, 9–15, fill in the missing information in the numbered space using a word, number or letters.

After you have listened once, replay the recording.

You have ten seconds to read through the notes.

[pause]

Now listen, and fill in the missing information.

Woman: Hello, Wilson's Office Supplies.
Man: Hello, this is Gillmann International. I'm afraid the desk you delivered last week is too large. Could I change it for a smaller one?

Woman: Yes, certainly. What is the name again?
Man: Gillmann International, spelt G-I-double L-M-A-double N.
Woman: Right. What's the date of that order?
Man: The invoice is dated the fifth of July . . . I can give you the order number: DT one, nine, oh, double five.
Woman: Yes, here it is. Have you a copy of our catalogue there? You ordered the hundred and thirty-seven point five centimetre desk, didn't you?
Man: Yes, that desk is too wide. It's the smaller one I need – one hundred and thirty-one centimetres wide.
Woman: Yes, that's reference number ZY double eight-three-two-oh.
Man: Yes, fine. And could you collect the other one when you deliver the new desk?
Woman: Yes. This desk is cheaper, it's a hundred and seventy-nine pounds ninety-nine . . . so that'll be . . . a hundred and sixty-two pounds with your normal ten-per-cent discount.
Man: Good. Could you credit our account?
Woman: Yes, that'll be twenty-seven pounds. We could deliver the new desk next Thursday, the fourteenth, or the following week on the nineteenth.
Man: Um, the later date is best. You've got our address.
Woman: Yes. We'll put the credit through after delivery.
Man: Good. Thanks for your help . . .

[pause]

Now listen to the recording again.

[pause]

That is the end of Part Two. You now have ten seconds to check your answers.

[pause]

Part Three. Questions 16 to 22.

Look at the notes below.

Some information is missing.

You will hear a man giving a presentation about Arlington Park, a training centre for managers.

For each question, 16–22, fill in the missing information in the numbered space using one or two words.

After you have listened once, replay the recording.

You have ten seconds to look at the form.

[pause]

Now listen, and complete the form.

Man: Hello, everyone. Thank you for coming to hear about Arlington Park. Some of you know a lot about it already, but for people who don't, the first thing to say is that if you do want to see what sort of work we do, on every third Thursday in the month, there's an exhibition, so come along to that – you're very welcome.

At Arlington Park, we aim to help you not only to get the most out of your staff, but also the most out of you yourself. Our next two weekend workshops are covering two very important areas in this field: on the tenth of June, we have a workshop on communication. Nothing could be easier in our modern world and yet nothing is more difficult, too. On the seventeenth of July, we have a change in the programme; we previously advertised a course on using technology, but that day is now set aside for a course called simply 'Leadership', run by one of our best trainers, Richard Gordon. You probably know his management books.

The one-day weekend workshops are just one of the types of courses we offer. We also offer three-day programmes, and these include accommodation. I'll leave a pile of leaflets about those with you, so that you can look at them at your leisure.

Arlington Park is very well equipped, and managers always enjoy their stay. Our facilities are excellent, and we have special training suites, as well as a fitness centre.

Every quarter, we publish a magazine – I've got a few copies here for those of you who haven't seen it before. We've just changed the name; it used to be *Developing People*, now it's called *Moving Forward*. The articles in it are written by the trainers and by the managers attending our courses.

If anyone would like to go on our mailing list, would you please fill in one of these enquiry forms and leave it at reception? I'll pick up all the forms at the end of the morning. Now, onto more detail . . .

[pause]

Now listen to the recording again.

[pause]

That is the end of Part Three. You now have twenty seconds to check your answers.

[pause]

Key

Part Four. Questions 23 to 30.

You will hear an interview with John Winterman, the Managing Director of a sports-equipment manufacturing company called Turners.

For each question, 23–30, mark one letter (A, B or C) for the correct answer.

After you have listened once, replay the recording.

You now have forty-five seconds to read through the questions.

[pause]

Now listen, and mark A, B or C.

Woman: . . . and this morning, we welcome John Winterman, Managing Director of Turners, the sports company which manufactures golf and tennis equipment.

Man: Morning.

Woman: So, John, you took charge of the company after a management buy-out. What made you and the other managers sure that it would be a successful move?

Man: Well, when we bought the business in nineteen ninety-seven, we knew there were financial problems to solve, including some hidden debts. But we felt the products themselves were really excellent, and a good basis from which to grow the company. And, although the brand image wasn't particularly well known, we felt it was possible to build on it.

Woman: I see. I believe the previous owners weren't specialists in the field . . .

Man: That's right . . . they were a large engineering group called AFT.

Woman: Did that cause any difficulties?

Man: Yes. Although AFT used the same management systems as in its other – engineering – businesses, and these seemed to be working, the production system just wasn't right for a consumer goods company. Turners offers a wide range of products, and has a complex business mix as a result.

Woman: I see. And how did their management system affect distribution?

Man: Well, the first thing we realised was that, although there was an up-to-date computer system, it was impossible to follow the movement of products around the world. The items we manufactured had a different product number in each country! The methods of transport also varied enormously from one country to another, which made the invoices complicated.

Woman: And what sort of service was the customer getting?

Man: Well, it wasn't very efficient. Our customers, the sports outlets, complained that although they were usually on time, orders often had items missing. I think these outlets only stayed with us because there was still demand for our products.

Woman: And how do you intend to promote the brand?

Man: Well, with sports equipment, image is all important, because there's so much competition. Although AFT had been active in their promotions with sports clubs in the early days, they hadn't kept up their efforts. Consequently, many players, especially those still at schools, are unfamiliar with our name. Our aim now is to make Turners products a big name at all the important sports events across the world.

Woman: What was your approach to reorganising the company?

Man: Well, the first thing we did was appoint new directors.

Woman: And where did you start?

Man: Well, we knew we had to spend money on marketing, but the most important thing was to introduce better management control of finances, and after that, to look very carefully at the organisation and cost of manufacturing.

Woman: Did you make any changes there?

Man: Oh, yes. To take one example, at one point we started out manufacturing tennis balls in Germany. But costs were lower in the Philippines. So in the end, we moved all our manufacturing there. By the end of this year, ninety-five per cent of our production will be there, although we are opening one small plant in Indonesia, too.

Woman: And is the company on a better financial basis now?

Man: Absolutely. We'll be in profit this year, and looking to expand.

Woman: You plan to introduce new products, then?

Man: Yes. We've just launched a new product, a waterproof tennis ball, and we've signed contracts with several players from different countries to give us an international image, so I'm really pleased about that. But our key objective is to develop the products we have, such as tennis rackets, and improve them further.

Woman: So the future looks promising.
Man: It certainly does.
Woman: Thanks, John.
Man: Thank you.

[pause]

Now listen to the recording again.

[pause]

That is the end of Part Four. You now have ten minutes to transfer your answers to your Answer Sheet.

[pause]

Note: Teacher, stop the recording here and time ten minutes. Remind students when there is **one** minute remaining.

That is the end of the test.

Test 2 Reading

Part 1

1 B   2 C   3 B   4 B   5 C

Part 2

6 F   7 H   8 D   9 B   10 C

Part 3

11 C   12 D   13 E   14 H   15 F

Part 4

16 B   17 B   18 A   19 C   20 C
21 A   22 B

Part 5

23 A   24 B   25 C   26 C   27 A
28 A

Part 6

29 A   30 B   31 B   32 C   33 B
34 C   35 A   36 C   37 A   38 C
39 B   40 A

Part 7

41 PRIMASCAN
42 (DINNER) INVITATION(S) / INVITATION CARD(S)
43 (1ST) AUG(UST) (2009)
44 150
45 (MR) MARTIN ADAMS

Test 2 Writing

Part 1

Sample A

> Jorge Ruiz who is my new client will arrive at my office at 2:00pm tomorrow. I am afraid that I might be late because of a meeting conference at 1:30pm. Could you please recept her and tell her waitting for me? Thank you.

Band 4
A good attempt at the task set. All three content points are covered, but a little effort is required by the reader when processing the third point.

Sample B

> Helen:
> I want to telling about new client Jorge Ruiz arriving to our office in the tomorrow afternoon at 2 o'clock. I hope you don't be late. You may welcome to Mr Ruiz's visit.

Band 2
An inadequate attempt at the task set. The task has been partly misunderstood, so the script contains noticeable irrelevance. Only the first point is dealt with.

Part 2

Sample C

> Dear Ms Dalton
>
> I am writing in reference to your letter. Our company is a software developer and we are interested in your product. We want to offer our workers a better comfort.
>
> Would there be any kind of discount if we make a big order? If it is possible, I would like your representative to come before the end of the month. Please make sure he comes from 9am to 1pm.
>
> Yours sincerely,
>
> Human Resources Manager

Band 5
This represents a full realisation of the task set. All four content points are covered. The language used

Key

is confident and natural, and the script is organised effectively. It would have a very positive effect on the reader.

Sample D

> Dear Ms Dalton. Thank you for your letter. Our company sales computer monitors. In fact she is interested by your product. Your price is hight.
>
> We are interesting by your screen but we must have a discount price. Because we sale a lot monitors. We ask a discount of the price. We propose that meet you Monday or Thuesday for a demonstration. If you agree, please confirm.
>
> I look forward to hearing from you.
>
> Ms D
>
> Office Manager

Band 3
The second content point is not covered, but this represents a reasonable attempt at the task set. Although they are not consistently successful, register and cohesion are satisfactory on the whole. A number of errors are present, but overall there is an adequate range of structures and vocabulary.

Test 2 Listening

Part 1

1 C   2 A   3 A   4 C   5 A   6 B
7 B   8 A

Part 2

9 (WWW.) AXIBIZ (.CO.UK)
10 (£) 18.75
11 26 (CM) (BY 30 CM)
12 GOLD
13 (07950) 332841
14 4.30 / HALF PAST FOUR
15 5(TH) (APRIL)

Part 3

16 INTERNET ADVERTISING
17 HILL
18 (NEW) CONTACTS
19 VIDEO CAMERA(S)
20 NEW YORK / NY

21 OCT(OBER)
22 DISCOUNT(S)

Part 4

23 B   24 C   25 A   26 B   27 C
28 A   29 C   30 A

Tapescript

Listening Test 2

This is the Business English Certificate Preliminary 4, Listening Test 2.

Part One. Questions 1 to 8.

For questions 1–8, you will hear eight short recordings. For each question, mark one letter (A, B or C) for the correct answer.

Here is an example: What time does the man expect to arrive at the meeting?

[pause]

Man: Hello, Liz. It's Mark. I'm still at the airport. The plane's delayed. I was supposed to be at the meeting at twelve thirty, but I'm probably not going to make it until thirteen thirty. We're not scheduled to take off for another hour yet, so won't land till eleven forty-five at the earliest.
Woman: Don't worry. I'll send your apologies.

[pause]

The answer is C.

Now we are ready to start.

After you have listened once, replay each recording.

[pause]

One: Which graph is the man talking about?

[pause]

Man: The year started quite slowly, but sales in the second quarter picked up well. Although there was a slight drop in the third quarter, I'm pleased to say that sales started to rise again at the end of the year.

[pause]

Two: Which jobs will be created when the company relocates?

[pause]

Woman: Family Fashions is relocating part of its mail-order operation, with the creation of two hundred jobs in Manchester. All jobs at the current packing centre will remain, and deliveries will operate as before. The new customer-service staff will work at a purpose-built site, very close . . .

[pause]

Three: Why are the brochures late?

[pause]

Man: It's the printers here . . . I'm sorry your brochures are late, we've had some problems.
Woman: Not your new machinery?
Man: Something else this time . . . some of our drivers have been ill this week. We've sent your order by post – we thought it would be quicker, as we've only got a few delivery vans going out.
Woman: OK, thanks.

[pause]

Four: What will Mediband's new owners do?

[pause]

Woman: I hear there has been a takeover of Mediband.
Man: Yes . . . it was running at a loss.
Woman: How did the workforce react? I expect they were worried about their jobs.
Man: Well, actually, the new parent group's announced plans to increase the company's output and market more products abroad. So their future's secure now.

[pause]

Five: When will the sales conference be held?

[pause]

Man: We'll have to move the sales conference, I'm afraid. It's scheduled for Wednesday the twenty-fifth of November, but there's a trade fair in Amsterdam the following day that senior staff are attending.
Woman: We could move it to Monday the thirtieth . . .?
Man: Mmm . . . actually, better to bring it forward to Monday the twenty-third . . . A pity about the twenty-fifth, though – it seemed a good day for everyone.

[pause]

Six: Which chart shows exports of mobile phones this year?

[pause]

Man: Mobile phone sales have remained steady overall this year, though the export market shares have changed. Now Europe and the United States together account for the same amount as South-East Asia.

[pause]

Seven: Which day is the meeting arranged for?

[pause]

Man: Would you be able to attend a meeting next week?
Woman: Monday would be OK, but I may have to cancel an appointment. Er, Tuesday or Wednesday mornings are possible.
Man: Shall we say Tuesday rather than Monday?
Woman: That's probably the easiest thing. Then I won't have to change my arrangements for Monday, and I'd like it earlier than Wednesday, really.

[pause]

Eight: Why is the man phoning the suppliers?

[pause]

Woman: Please leave your message after the tone.
Man: Hello, Lars here from Olaffsens. About the tool component you supplied last month – the CX two seven . . . We've found we're getting more faults than usual, so I want you to look at the part again and perhaps adjust the measurements. Could you call me as soon as possible?

[pause]

That is the end of Part One.

[pause]

Part Two. Questions 9 to 15.

Look at the notes below.

Some information is missing.

You will hear a man giving some information about gifts to order for staff who have performed well.

For each question, 9–15, fill in the missing information in the numbered space using a word, numbers or letters.

131

Key

After you have listened once, replay the recording.

You have ten seconds to read through the notes.

[pause]

Now listen, and fill in the missing information.

Man: Emma, Mark here. I'm calling to tell you about the annual performance prizes for senior staff.
Woman: OK, let me know the details of the order.
Man: You can order them all from one website. It's www.axibiz.co.uk.
Woman: Is that A-X-I-B-U-S?
Man: It's A-X-I-B-I-Z. OK? We need fifteen silver calculators . . .
Woman: How will I know which ones?
Man: There are two designs. We want the eighteen pound seventy-five ones, rather than the twenty-one pound seventy-five ones.
Woman: Right. What else?
Man: Leather picture holders . . . but they come in different sizes. The larger ones are twenty-nine by thirty-one centimetres. Get the other ones. They're twenty-six by thirty. We'll need five of those at forty-two pounds.
Woman: What's the star-performance prize?
Man: It's the ninety-five-pound Gold Gift Desk Set.
Woman: Is that the exact name?
Man: Yes. And that's all. Call my mobile to let me know about the order. I'll be out of the office tomorrow.
Woman: I don't have your number.
Man: I always forget it. Um . . . Oh yes, oh-seven-nine-five-oh, double three-two-eight-four-one. Try to call before one thirty tomorrow.
Woman: Ah, I'm in meetings till two. Can I call you afterwards?
Man: Sure. Make it before four thirty.
Woman: Fine. When's the order got to arrive by?
Man: Very soon. The presentations are on the seventh of April.
Woman: Next month?
Man: Yes, so the fifth at the latest.
Woman: I'll do what I can.

[pause]

Now listen to the recording again.

[pause]

That is the end of Part Two. You now have ten seconds to check your answers.

[pause]

Part Three. Questions 16 to 22.

Look at the notes below about a marketing conference.

Some information is missing.

You will hear part of a report to colleagues about the marketing conference.

For each question, 16–22, fill in the missing information in the numbered space using one or two words.

After you have listened once, replay the recording.

You have ten seconds to look at the notes.

[pause]

Now listen, and complete the notes.

Man: As you know, I attended the annual marketing conference in Manchester last week. As always, it was very useful. There were some first-rate seminars and presentations. I was particularly impressed by a talk on internet advertising. In fact, I plan to ask the speaker to come and do a workshop for our staff here. Her name's Susan Hill; some of you may have heard of her – she writes regularly for a number of business magazines. Conferences aren't just about seminars and workshops, though. In fact, I'd say that for most people, and I include myself, probably the most important part of any conference are the new contacts you make.
    One very useful person I met at the Manchester conference was a man called Harry Baxter, from a company in Glasgow. He'd already heard of our video cameras and wanted to know more about them. Anyway, he's interested in placing an order for them with us; he'll be confirming that in the next couple of days.
    I also met two people from an American firm called Bentley High-Tech. They're a major supplier to stores all over the USA. Their headquarters are in New York. They seem really impressed by what we're doing. In fact, one of them intends to come over to spend a few days with us in October. He might like to see something of our manufacturing process and production capacity, though I think he's mainly interested in discounts. If all goes well, this could lead to a really major contract for us.
    One of the other aspects of the conference that . . .

[pause]

Now listen to the recording again.

[pause]

That is the end of Part Three. You now have twenty seconds to check your answers.

[pause]

Part Four. Questions 23 to 30.

You will hear a radio interview with a successful businessman called Nigel Player, who runs an airline on the island of Alderney.

For each question, 23–30, mark one letter (A, B or C) for the correct answer.

After you have listened once, replay the recording.

You now have forty-five seconds to read through the questions.

[pause]

Now listen, and mark A, B or C.

Woman: This week's Business Profile looks at the career of Nigel Player. Good afternoon, Nigel.
Man: Good afternoon.
Woman: Nigel, you now own a very successful small airline on the island of Alderney, but have you always worked in transport?
Man: Well, actually my career's been very varied and I moved into transport quite recently. I started work at a bank, where I was responsible for dealing with investments. I then moved into electronics, where I ran a multi-million-pound company.
Woman: So, why did you leave such an important job and go to Alderney?
Man: Initially, I had no intention of leaving. I just wanted some free time before returning to the company. I originally planned to spend a year doing a book on successful businesses while staying with a friend who had retired there.
Woman: But Alderney is a very small island quite a long way off the south coast of England. I imagine you soon got bored.
Man: That's right. It's beautiful there, but within two weeks, I was looking around for some kind of business opportunity. I'd already noticed that food prices were high and service was poor, so I decided to try food retailing. I bought an old general store – it wasn't cheap, but I was optimistic about its potential. I modernised and expanded the premises and opened in October nineteen ninety-nine.
Woman: But that's still very different from owning an airline!
Man: Yes, but the problem on an island like Alderney is that the best way to get fresh produce is to fly it in. That was fine during the winter months, but in summer, when there were lots of tourists wanting to come to the island, the local airline sometimes used to just leave my food on the mainland and bring tourists instead – carrying passengers earns them far more money than carrying freight, of course.
Woman: So, what did you decide to do to solve the problem?
Man: Well, I thought about bringing things in by boat. It wouldn't cost so much and might be more reliable, even in bad weather, but it would take much longer. That's when I decided I had no choice but to buy my own small eight-seater plane. Soon I was bringing in food twice daily.
Woman: But that was just carrying freight?
Man: At first, yes, but my supermarket customers kept asking me to find a place for them on my plane. I realised there was a great demand for competitive prices, so I put together a business plan for operating a small passenger airline twice a week. It was a challenge, but I really enjoyed doing something so different.
Woman: So was it difficult getting everything prepared?
Man: Well, of course I already had quite a bit of business experience, and a good friend of mine was involved in the transport business for years and he gave me a lot of advice. But the main thing really was that I'd already had a year's experience of flying and transporting goods, so I understood about regulations and so on. The company got its licence, and we made our first flight in January two thousand and two. In the first month, we carried thirty-eight passengers, but by the end of the year, we had totalled eight thousand.
Woman: So, what would you say is the secret of your success?
Man: I think it helps that we're a small company running a purely local service. If a big airline upsets a hundred customers, there are millions more willing to use them. If we have eight unhappy people on one of our morning flights, the whole island knows about it by the evening. So all our staff are very committed to giving a good personal service.
Woman: Thank you, Nigel. That was very interesting . . .

[pause]

Key

Now listen to the recording again.

[pause]

That is the end of Part Four. You now have ten minutes to transfer your answers to your Answer Sheet.

[pause]

Note: Teacher, stop the recording here and time ten minutes. Remind students when there is **one** minute remaining

That is the end of the test.

Test 3   Reading

Part 1

1 A   2 C   3 C   4 A   5 A

Part 2

6 H   7 F   8 E   9 D   10 C

Part 3

11 C   12 H   13 D   14 A   15 G

Part 4

16 A   17 C   18 A   19 C   20 B
21 A   22 B

Part 5

23 B   24 C   25 C   26 B   27 C
28 A

Part 6

29 C   30 B   31 A   32 A   33 B
34 C   35 C   36 A   37 B   38 C
39 B   40 B

Part 7

41 (MR) TONY MOSS
42 REGAL HOTEL
43 7–9 (TH) (AUGUST)
44 BUFFET LUNCH
45 SALES (DEPARTMENT)

Test 3   Writing
Part 1
Sample A

> To: All staff
>
> Subject: Working hours
>
> In the first week of September the working hours will change. All staff will work from 9:00AM to 16:00PM, and each employement is able to choose his free day. I decided to do this change because a lots Staff's people complained about working hours.

Band 4
A good attempt at the task. All the content points have been covered, but a little effort is required by the reader.

Sample B

> Our working time in the afternoon will change from 14:00–17:00 to 15:00–18:00. This is due to the arrival of summer so we'd better leave more time for rest in the noon. The new timetable will take effect next week.

Band 5
This is a very good attempt at the task set. All points are fully covered.

Part 2
Sample C

> Dear Mr Morgan
>
> Thank you for your letter. We need a new delivery company because we want to have staideble partner. We need deliviring new equipment for computers. But all details I want to say.

Band 2
Only two points successfully addressed, and the response is also very short at only 35 words.

134

Sample D

> Dear Mr Morgan,
>
> Thank you for your letter.
>
> I beleive there is a great opportunity for us because the delivery company we'd been working before has gone bankrupt, so we're looking for a new one.
>
> Let me explain what type of goods we usually need to deliver. We run a small on-line shop in the Internet offering different types of hardware like personal computers and various networking eqipement.
>
> Currently we're expanding in the local market so we're interested in a long-term partnership with a delivery service, like yours.
>
> Could you please think of a suitable day to visit our office?
>
> I look forward to your reply!
>
> Best regards,
>
> Mr P,
>
> CEO

Band 5
This is a full representation of the task set. All the content points are achieved, and the language used is confident and natural. It would have a very positive effect on the reader.

Test 3   Listening

Part 1

1 B   2 A   3 B   4 A   5 B   6 B
7 A   8 B

Part 2

9 (JANE) ROTHWELL
10 (£) 166 (MILLION) (POUNDS)
11 327 (PENCE / P)
12 11 (% / PER CENT)
13 52 (PRODUCT LINES)
14 16,000 (SQUARE METRES)
15 33 (%)

Part 3

16 (A) TRAINING (COMPANY)
17 STAR CONSULTANTS
18 GRADUATES
19 (GIVING) PRESENTATIONS
20 PROMOTING PRODUCTS
21 MICROPHONE / MIKE
22 PROBLEMS

Part 4

23 B   24 B   25 C   26 B   27 C
28 A   29 B   30 A

Tapescript

Listening Test 3

This is the Business English Certificate Preliminary 4, Listening Test 3.

Part One. Questions 1 to 8.

For questions 1–8, you will hear eight short recordings. For each question, mark one letter (A, B or C) for the correct answer.

Here is an example: Who is Anna going to write to?

[pause]

Man: Anna, that supplier we use has become very unreliable, and we've decided to look for another one.
Woman: Seems a good idea.
Man: We don't need to inform our clients, but could you send a note round to all our departments when we've decided who to replace the supplier with?
Woman: Yes, of course.

[pause]

The answer is A.

Now we are ready to start.

After you have listened once, replay each recording.

[pause]

One: When will the next meeting be?

[pause]

Man: Hi, Sarah, John here.
Woman: Morning.
Man: Can we fix a meeting next week to discuss the report you gave me? . . . I'm out of the office until Wednesday the twenty-third, so how about Thursday the twenty-fourth at ten?
Woman: Hmm. The morning of the twenty-fifth would be better . . .
Man: Sorry, I'm already booked then.
Woman: OK then, Thursday it is.

Key

[pause]

Two: Which of the goods were delivered?

[pause]

Woman: Office Wholesalers.
Man: Hello, it's Mark here from Greens Office Supplies – it's about our order. We ordered one thousand folders and five hundred pens and the same number of pencils. They were supposed to be delivered this morning, but we're still waiting for the pens and the folders.
Woman: Oh, I'm sorry. The other items will be sent out this afternoon, though. We only got them in about an hour ago.
Man: Thanks.

[pause]

Three: Why is the man apologising?

[pause]

Man: Morning, Nicky. Did you tell the others that I'd be late? Train again . . .
Woman: Where's the report you were going to leave me? It's missing, and I need to read it before the meeting.
Man: Oh, Mike asked for it, so I passed it to him.
Woman: But that was confidential information!
Man: Oh, I didn't realise. I'm sorry. I promise it won't happen again.

[pause]

Four: What is the cover of the new brochure like?

[pause]

Man: Have you seen the design for the cover of the new brochure?
Woman: Yes, I have.
Man: What's it like?
Woman: It's just a world map.
Man: Nothing exciting, then?
Woman: Well, it's better than last year's, with that photo of head office!
Man: And the company name in big letters along the top.
Woman: That runs down the side of the cover this time – much more original!

[pause]

Five: Which chart is correct?

[pause]

Man: And here are the numbers of hours lost to staff illness. As expected, January was our worst month, with many people off sick. February wasn't too bad; only half as many hours lost. March was excellent, but April was disappointing.

[pause]

Six: What are the staff still forgetting to do with company cars?

[pause]

Man: . . . and I see there are *still* problems with staff borrowing company cars!
Woman: I sent out memos reminding them to write down how far they'd driven.
Man: Mmm, that's fine now. I wanted a car for an important trip last week, though, and there was no fuel in it. Staff *know* they mustn't leave cars empty. But at least they do tidy up inside them now.

[pause]

Seven: What do the speakers say about Esther Wong?

[pause]

Man: Do you know who got the Project Manager post?
Woman: No idea. But I know Esther Wong was turned down.
Man: That's a surprise . . . She's the most senior person in the department, isn't she?
Woman: Yes. She certainly expected to get it – she's actually given in her notice because she thought it was unfair.
Man: Oh well . . . She won't have much trouble finding something else.

[pause]

Eight: Which chart is the speaker talking about?

[pause]

Man: We invested heavily in production, as we had to update the factory. We put about a quarter of our investment into a strong marketing campaign, which was supported by a slightly larger investment in the sales team.

[pause]

That is the end of Part One.

[pause]

Part Two. Questions 9 to 15.

Look at the notes below.

Some information is missing.

You will hear a journalist talking to the Head of Public Relations of a large supermarket chain.

For each question, 9–15, fill in the missing information in the numbered space using a word, numbers or letters.

After you have listened once, replay the recording.

You have ten seconds to read through the notes.

[pause]

Now listen, and fill in the missing information.

Man: Hello, Bill Isaacs . . .
Woman: Hello. This is Fiona Holiday from the *Financial News*. I'm writing an article about the success of the Rezzo supermarket chain.
Man: Great – well, business has improved here since the arrival of our new Chief Executive, Jane Rothwell . . .
Woman: Sorry, that's Jane . . .?
Man: Rothwell . . . that's R-O-T-H-W-E-double L.
Woman: Thanks. Now, let's talk about your current position – I believe Rezzo's have just announced their pre-tax profits . . .
Man: Yes, and the latest figures are one hundred and sixty-six million pounds for the six months to the end of September . . . that's up eight million from the previous six months.
Woman: What will that mean for shareholders?
Man: Very good news – shares have actually more than doubled since March, from one hundred and fifty pence to three hundred and twenty-seven . . .
Woman: I see. So what are your sales figures like?
Man: Well, sales per square metre are up eleven per cent . . . That's two per cent better than forecast.
Woman: Mm-hm . . . and how was that achieved?
Man: Well, we've increased the number of special discounts we offer on product lines from twenty-eight to fifty-two.
Woman: So, do Rezzo's have plans to expand?
Man: Absolutely. We're going to open two sixteen-thousand-square-metre hypermarket stores in January, and a further five or six are planned over the year.
Woman: I see.
Man: And thirty-three per cent of the selling space in the new hypermarkets will be used for non-food items . . . that's up from twenty-five per cent in the existing supermarkets.
Woman: Interesting. Thanks, Mr Isaacs, that's all I need.
Man: Thank you.

[pause]

Now listen to the recording again.

[pause]

That is the end of Part Two. You now have ten seconds to check your answers.

[pause]

Part Three. Questions 16 to 22.

Look at the notes below.

Some information is missing.

You will hear a man giving a talk about his work and career.

For each question, 16–22, fill in the missing information in the numbered space using one or two words.

After you have listened once, replay the recording.

You have ten seconds to read through the notes.

[pause]

Now listen, and fill in the missing information.

Man: Good morning, everyone. Thank you for inviting me here today. My name's Patrick Greene, and I've had quite an interesting and varied career.

I actually spent nearly ten years as an actor before I went into business with a friend. We set up a training company. As you can imagine, that brought me into contact with a lot of different organisations, and I soon realised that new employees were often asked to give talks very early in their career, and that it was something they found extremely difficult. As a result, I sold my share of the business and started my current company, which is called Star Consultants.

We offer courses in public speaking – they're designed for graduates. My acting experience was very useful, and I had some coaching myself before I started courses for other people. There is a great need in companies for staff who can communicate well, and I can help people to feel confident about those skills.

There are two main courses I offer. The first is called 'Giving Presentations'. I actually help with the technical side of things, as well as the necessary speaking skills. The other course there is a great demand for is called 'Promoting Products', and I do a lot of training in this, too.

Key

The first part of any course is always voice work. I spend a lot of time getting people to produce a good, clear sound that an audience can hear easily. I then move on to how to speak with a microphone, since nearly all of my trainees have to use one. We then do a lot of practice, and trainees help each other.

The final part of the course then looks at different things, like how to deal with problems and how to time a talk.

Now, I've got a video here to show you of one of my courses in action . . .

[pause]

Now listen to the recording again.

[pause]

That is the end of Part Three. You now have twenty seconds to check your answers.

[pause]

Part Four. Questions 23 to 30.

You will hear an interview between a radio presenter and a businessman, Tim Black, about British people relocating and going to work outside the UK.

For each question, 23–30, mark one letter (A, B or C) for the correct answer.

After you have listened once, replay the recording.

You now have forty-five seconds to read through the questions.

[pause]

Now listen, and mark A, B or C.

Woman: And today I'm talking to Tim Black, who has recently returned to the UK from working abroad. He is currently working on a report about relocation and its effect on companies and employees. Tim, what kind of people are sent abroad by their companies?

Man: Well, generally speaking, if you're relatively senior in a company, you have a good chance, and also if you've worked abroad before and have shown you're adaptable. But my company always looks particularly for people with skills which might be needed in their work overseas, and that's how I got my chance to go.

Woman: I see, but what about the general situation? I've heard that fewer employees are sent abroad now than in the past. Why is that?

Man: Well, some Human Resources departments are thinking much harder about how many staff they can relocate, and companies are only taking the best candidates from the UK, while filling other positions locally. That's because they know that relocation is expensive. They don't always want to invest in it, which is a pity, as the experience can equip people with skills that lead to promotion.

Woman: So, what's the position with British workers?

Man: Well, it seems that people are happier to relocate to another area of the UK rather than go to another country. It's especially popular to go and live outside the big cities and commute in to work – although, as far as London is concerned, in the last few years, companies already based in the countryside have found it increasingly easy to attract staff away from the capital.

Woman: Mm. Now, for people considering relocation abroad, are there financial arrangements to be made before leaving?

Man: Yes. You may want to check that any health insurance you have is still valid. Oh, and one very important point is to find out what will happen to payments into your pension fund while you are abroad. You need to make sure that these will continue. Um, also, you may want to rent out your house while you're away. It's best to use a rental agency to do this, so that they can sort out any problems in your absence.

Woman: Now, you've worked abroad, in Dubai. What work was your company involved in there?

Man: We'd got a contract from an international bank there. A firm in the UK had designed an office block for them, and we went to Dubai to arrange for the purchase of the materials and to build it. I was part of the team involved in the project, in partnership with a local firm.

Woman: And how did your company help you decide whether or not to go?

Man: They made it very easy for me. They paid for me to go and see the place to decide if it would suit me. I then asked a colleague at the branch in Dubai to help me with my move there, and he was excellent. Sadly, though, the Arabic language lessons I'd requested never happened!

Woman: Oh, that's a pity. And what about accommodation?

Man: Well, buying a house there was going to be very expensive, so another colleague offered to help me move to an apartment owned by my company, which I was very grateful for. Finding accommodation can be difficult when you first arrive.

Woman: And you stayed in Dubai for three years – quite a long time. Is that the usual length of relocation in your company?

Man: Anything over a year is considered a long-term assignment, and three years is normal for international relocations because of the cost involved. My job there was to manage the progress of our project, so it was likely to be long term. But I enjoyed the experience, and learnt a lot from it, even though it was a familiar area of work to me.

Woman: Well, Tim, thank you for talking to us.

[pause]

Now listen to the recording again.

[pause]

That is the end of Part Four. You now have ten minutes to transfer your answers to your Answer Sheet.

[pause]

Note: Teacher, stop the recording here and time ten minutes. Remind students when there is **one** minute remaining.

That is the end of the test.

Test 4 Reading

Part 1

1 B   2 A   3 B   4 C   5 C

Part 2

6 G   7 D   8 B   9 F   10 A

Part 3

11 F   12 A   13 G   14 C   15 D

Part 4

16 A   17 B   18 C   19 C   20 A
21 A   22 B

Part 5

23 B   24 A   25 A   26 C   27 C
28 B

Part 6

29 C   30 C   31 A   32 B   33 C
34 B   35 C   36 B   37 A   38 B
39 C   40 A

Part 7

41 (MRS / MS / MISS) ANDREA HARLOCK
42 (THE) FINANCE MANAGER
43 (TUESDAY) 11(TH) JULY (2008)
44 FUNDING GROWTH
45 (A) PARKING (SPACE)

Test 4 Writing

Part 1

Sample A

> I'm apologising but I cannot help you to write your report.
>
> I know one person who could be interested on your work because he had experience on German market. The name is Lorenzo Maio
>
> Phone 0349027451
>
> Gaia

Band 3

The first content point is not covered, as the candidate does not give a reason why he/she cannot help Marina Walker with her report.

Sample B

> Dear Marina,
>
> I am writing to inform you that I'm not able to help you with the report you mentioned because I am preparing a meeting at the moment. Please ask Chris, the German student for help.
>
> Kind regards
>
> Maja

Band 5

This is a very good attempt at the task set, achieving all content points. No effort is required by the reader.

Key

Part 2
Sample C

> Dear Ms kranz,
>
> Thank you very much for your letter of 1 December. I would like to tell you that
>
> I will take the flight CA213 and will arrive at the airport at 9:00am on 5 December. Besides, I am very interesting in the production lines in your factory, may
>
> I have a visit?
>
> I will greatly thanks if you have a hotel accommodation for me.
>
> Your sincerely
>
> Pill

Band 4
All four content points are covered. This is a good realisation of the task set, which would have a positive effect on the reader. The register is appropriate on the whole, and there are no impeding errors.

Sample D

> Dear Ms Kranz:
>
> I'm hearing from you. Thank you very much. Please attention to my flight details number is 6768 on 15th Dec. at 9a.m.
>
> Because I will know about your products why they are very popular. I think I am going to visit your factory. If you will allow I think I will be meet your product manager.
>
> Please he will tells me about his experience and he thinks good method.
>
> At last. I will need a parking space but accommodation is the nearest your factory. I think I am going to your factory so easy Thanks.
>
> See you at the airport.
>
> Your good friend
>
> Sadie.

Band 2
The first three content points are covered, but the answer contains numerous errors, several of which impede. The content is not clearly organised or linked, which leads to confusion on the part of the reader.

Test 4 Listening

Part 1
1 C   2 B   3 A   4 C   5 B   6 C
7 C   8 A

Part 2
9 (JAMES) MCDOUGALL
10 35 (CM)
11 196 (DOTS PER CM)
12 20 (PAGES PER MINUTE)
13 HY1874
14 (£) 304 (POUNDS)
15 (FRIDAY) 16(TH) DEC(EMBER)

Part 3
16 NEW DEVELOPMENTS
17 TOWN HALL
18 EMPLOYMENT (LAW)
19 (DR JAMES) BLACK
20 SUPPLIERS
21 FUTURE PLANNING
22 DIRECTOR (OF WESTWICK BUSINESS SCHOOL)

Part 4
23 C   24 A   25 C   26 B   27 C
28 B   29 A   30 A

Tapescript

Listening Test 4

This is the Business English Certificate Preliminary 4, Listening Test 4.

Part One. Questions 1 to 8.

For questions 1–8, you will hear eight short recordings. For each question, mark one letter (A, B or C) for the correct answer.

Here is an example: What time does the man expect to arrive at the meeting?

[pause]

Man: Hello, Liz. It's Mark. I'm still at the airport. The plane's delayed. I was supposed to be at the meeting at twelve thirty, but I'm probably not going to make it until thirteen thirty. We are not scheduled to take off for another hour yet, so won't land till eleven forty-five at the earliest.
Woman: Don't worry. I'll send your apologies.

[pause]

The answer is C.

Now we are ready to start.

After you have listened once, replay each recording.

[pause]

One: How many people attended the annual general meeting this year?

[pause]

Man: Sarah, you were at the AGM, weren't you? What were the numbers like? I heard they were expecting over a hundred and eighty people.
Woman: Oh, I read the report, and it said there were approximately two hundred and fifty there, which is a lot more than the last one, when there were just over a hundred.
Man: And what were the speakers like?

[pause]

Two: Where will the man go first?

[pause]

Man: Good morning. I'm starting a temporary job in the Production Department today . . . could you tell me where that is?
Woman: All new employees have to report to the Security Office before starting work, so I'll take you there and then show you into the Presentation Room . . . there's an introductory talk for new staff. You'll go to your departments at about ten.
Man: Thanks a lot.

[pause]

Three: Which brand is the market leader?

[pause]

Woman: There's big competition between the top three brands.
Man: Yes, Thomsen used to be the strongest, but now it's close between Landor and . . .
Woman: . . . Sodex. Yes, I think Thomsen have lost their position lately. Landor have over thirty per cent of the market share now.
Man: Yes, but Sodex have about five per cent *more* than that.
Woman: Hm. Thomsen need to gain a lot more to really compete.

[pause]

Four: What time will the woman get to Oxford?

[pause]

Woman: Hello, I need to get to Oxford for a meeting at ten thirty.
Man: There's a train at nine fifteen which will get you there at ten forty-five.
Woman: Isn't there an earlier one?
Man: Yes, but you'd have to change. It leaves at seven thirty, and you arrive at nine forty-five.
Woman: Oh no, that's no good. I'll get the other one and change my meeting time.

[pause]

Five: Where will the woman find the file?

[pause]

Woman: Hi, John. Have you got the file on MPG Holdings?
Man: No, I put it back on your desk yesterday afternoon.
Woman: Did you? Well, it's disappeared.
Man: Have you checked your briefcase?
Woman: Oh, that's it. I put it in there last night. I meant to put it in the filing cabinet this morning.

[pause]

Six: Which chart shows the sales of sports clothing this month?

[pause]

Woman: How's the new ladies' sportswear range selling?
Man: It's made a big difference. Sports clothing is usually only ten per cent of our total sales, but since we introduced the new range, clothing sales have more than doubled, to twenty-five per cent this month. Our strongest item is still sports equipment, though; it still makes up over fifty per cent of total sales.

[pause]

Seven: Which department will get the biggest budget next year?

[pause]

Man: What about this year's budget?
Woman: Well, we're investing a lot in the factory this year, because we're expecting an increase in sales.
Man: Aren't distribution costs going to go up, then?
Woman: Yes, so Distribution's going to get around half the budget, and Production will get twenty

141

Key

per cent for their new computer system, and Sales will have nearly thirty per cent.

[pause]

Eight: Which graph shows orders correctly?

[pause]

Man: Our strategy of holding prices level from the beginning of the year seems to have had results. After a dip in the middle of the year, orders rose steadily, even though our customer base didn't increase.

[pause]

That is the end of Part One.

[pause]

Part Two. Questions 9 to 15.

Look at the notes below.

Some information is missing.

You will hear a man making an enquiry about ordering a new printer.

For each question, 9–15, fill in the missing information in the numbered space using a word, numbers or letters.

After you have listened once, replay the recording.

You have ten seconds to look at the notes.

[pause]

Now listen, and fill in the missing information.

Woman: CIT Computers.
Man: Hello. I'm ringing from Davies and Baker, Accountants. I need some advice about office equipment.
Woman: Right. Could I just take your name first?
Man: Yes, I'm James McDougall. That's M-C-D-O-U-G-A-double L.
Woman: Thank you. Now, what exactly are you interested in?
Man: We need a new office printer, but I'm not sure which type.
Woman: Do you need anything special?
Man: We haven't much space, so no wider than thirty-five centimetres.
Woman: We've got some that size.
Man: What about printout quality?
Woman: You can choose either two hundred and thirty-five or one hundred and ninety-six dots per centimetre. One hundred and ninety-six is fine if you don't do much specialised printing.

Man: That'll be OK. How fast is it? We're a busy office.
Woman: Ten pages per minute, and you only have to wait fifteen seconds before the first page prints out. There's an upgraded model that'll be out next month. That does twenty pages per minute.
Man: That sounds ideal. So, what model is it?
Woman: It's the HY one-eight-seven-four.
Man: And the price?
Woman: Well, we've a special offer on at the moment. It costs three hundred and eighty pounds, but if you order today, we can give you a twenty-per-cent discount, which brings it down to just three hundred and four pounds.
Man: That sounds fine. Do you deliver? We're based in Burnham.
Woman: Fine, we deliver there on a Friday. We could do Friday the ninth of December . . . ?
Man: I'd prefer the sixteenth.
Woman: Right. Now, about the delivery, we'll be in touch . . .

[pause]

Now listen to the recording again.

[pause]

That is the end of Part Two. You now have ten seconds to check your answers.

[pause]

Part Three. Questions 16 to 22.

Look at the notes about one month's events in a city's business community.

Some information is missing.

You will hear part of a radio programme about business events.

For each question, 16–22, fill in the missing information in the numbered space using one or two words.

After you have listened once, replay the recording.

You have ten seconds to read through the notes.

[pause]

Now listen, and fill in the missing information.

Man: There are several things happening for members of the business community this month. Starting on Thursday June the twelfth, there's a two-day conference called 'New Developments', which brings together the city's most important business people with business leaders from across the country. The event takes place in the Town Hall and offers an interesting programme of speeches and seminars. Day one concentrates on how companies can raise money for joint ventures, and day two looks at employment law. The occasion will be both high-powered and entertaining, with speeches from well-known people, among them Michael Hill of KTC. Giving the key speech of the conference will be the senior partner of a city legal firm, Dr James Black.

The following Wednesday, June the eighteenth, there's an all-day event called 'Fast Forward'. This will be held at the Ocean Park Hotel, to bring together new members of the city's business community and introduce them to suppliers, in an attempt to build further business in the city. It'll also be a chance for members to generally improve their business skills.

Finally, on Friday June the twenty-seventh, there's a seminar called 'Future Planning', to be held at the City University. This is to help companies look at their financial arrangements and the possibility of floating their company, with the aim of securing long-term growth. The speaker will be Paul Miller, former Chairman of Fasttrack Holdings, who is now Director of Westwick Business School.

If you're interested in any of the events I've mentioned, ring oh-two-oh-two, oh-six-one-oh-three for details.

[pause]

Now listen to the recording again.

[pause]

That is the end of Part Three. You now have twenty seconds to check your answers.

[pause]

Part Four. Questions 23 to 30.

You will hear a discussion between Philip Michael, the Chief Executive of IKD, a design company, and a journalist from the business section of a national newspaper.

For each question, 23–30, mark one letter (A, B or C) for the correct answer.

After you have listened once, replay the recording.

You have forty-five seconds to read through the questions.

[pause]

Now listen, and mark A, B or C.

Woman: Hello, Mr Michael, thanks for talking to me today.

Man: Not at all.

Woman: Your company is located in such wonderful countryside. I expect your clients like coming here, don't they? Or do they find it difficult to get here?

Man: Actually, the transport links aren't too bad, but we very rarely see our customers in person. What they do like about it is that it's a pretty secret location and rather difficult to find. Our work is very confidential.

Woman: Ah yes. Your designs are beginning to make the designs of some of your competitors look rather old-fashioned. How do your designers work on their ideas? Is it all about technology?

Man: Technology is the biggest part. We certainly have no use for pencils and drawing boards like the old-style design studios. Our designers use the latest computer-aided design system. Ideas can be tested from all angles just by using the computer screen. However, we haven't stopped building models completely – we just put the design into a solid form using clay or foam at a later stage of the process.

Woman: Ah-ha. I know you have several important projects at the moment. Who is your biggest client?

Man: All our work's important to us. We're best known for designing bikes and motorbikes, but the company that keeps us busiest these days is a car producer. However, there are also hundreds of different household items that we've designed in the past.

Woman: Do you only use your own designers or do you ever look for new ideas, for example by using well-known artists on a freelance basis?

Man: We certainly do look for ideas outside the company, but not from freelancers – our work's too secret for that. It's a very competitive market. We're even competing with the in-house R&D teams of our client companies! However, just now, we're working with scientists at a university to develop an even better system for designing products through the latest computer and video systems.

Woman: What do you think it is that your customers value most about you? Is it just the fact that you use the latest technology?

Man: Well, not that alone. Good-quality design can be made by any number of different methods, not just ours. What our customers

Key

particularly like is that with the technology, we can work faster than our competitors. Design has traditionally been a very slow process – but not here. That doesn't mean we're cheap, it just means we can get the design to the client before anyone else can.

Woman: You're becoming well known for your designs, now, aren't you? Didn't one of your racing bikes recently win an award in a competition?

Man: Well, what actually happened was, it was judged by over fifty international biking magazines to be the best design, which meant that they all used it on their front covers, which was fantastic publicity for us, and hopefully the bike will go on to win lots of races.

Woman: It must be sad when designs are rejected. However successful a design company is, is it true that most designs never actually go into production?

Man: Usually, but not with us. Almost all our designs are put into production as soon as the company receives them. Our customers want designs not just to look at and think about for some later date, but to use immediately. Very few are rejected.

Woman: How do your customers pay you?

Man: Many design companies demand from their clients a share in the profits from sales of products made to their designs. That can be very costly to the client. Our customers pay us on a straight fee basis: one project, one fee. If it takes many more hours to produce than we had expected, that's our problem, but the client gets the project on time.

Woman: Well, you've certainly got a successful operation going . . .

[pause]

Now listen to the recording again.

[pause]

That is the end of Part Four. You now have ten minutes to transfer your answers to your Answer Sheet.

[pause]

Note: Teacher, stop the recording here and time ten minutes. Remind students when there is **one** minute remaining.

That is the end of the test.

INTERLOCUTOR FRAMES

To facilitate practice for the Speaking test, the scripts that the interlocutor follows for Parts 2 and 3 appear below. They should be used in conjunction with Tests 1–4 Speaking tasks. These tasks are contained in booklets in the real Speaking test.

Interlocutor frames are not included for Part 1, in which the interlocutor asks the candidates questions directly rather than asking them to perform tasks.

Part 2: Mini presentations for two candidates (about five minutes)

Interlocutor:
- Now, in this part of the test, I'm going to give each of you a choice of two different topics. I'd like you to choose one topic and give a short presentation on it for about a minute. You will have a minute to prepare this and you can make notes if you wish.
- All right? Here are your topics. Please don't write anything in the booklet.

[Interlocutor hands each candidate a booklet and a pencil and paper for notes.]

Interlocutor:
- Now, *B*, which topic have you chosen, A or B?
- Would you like to show *A* your task and tell us what you think is important when *[interlocutor states candidate's chosen topic]*?

[Candidate B speaks for one minute.]

Interlocutor:
- Thank you. Now, *A*, which do you think is most important, *[interlocutor reads out bullet points]*?
- Thank you. Now, *A*, which topic have you chosen, A or B?
- Would you like to show *B* your task and tell us what you think is important when *[interlocutor states candidate's chosen topic]*?

[Candidate A speaks for one minute.]

Interlocutor:
- Thank you. Now, *B*, which do you think is most important, *[interlocutor reads out bullet points]*?
- Thank you.
- Can I have the booklets, please?

Part 3: Collaborative task and discussion (about five minutes)

Interlocutor:
- Now, in this part of the test, you are going to talk about something together.
- I'm going to describe a situation.

  Example: The manufacturing company you work for wants to improve contacts with a local business college. Talk together for about two minutes about some of the ways the company could help the college and decide which two are best.

- Here are some ideas to help you.

[Interlocutor places the booklet in front of the candidates so that they can both see it.]

- I'll describe the situation again.

  Example: The manufacturing company you work for wants to improve contacts with a local business college. Talk together for about two minutes about some of the ways the company could help the college and decide which two are best.

  Now talk together. Please speak so that we can hear you.

[Candidates have about two minutes to complete the task.]

- Can I have the booklet, please?

[Interlocutor selects one or more of the following questions as appropriate.]

Examples:
- Can you think of any other things a company could do to help a local college? (Why?)
- How important do you think practical experience is for business students? (Why?/Why not?)
- What do you think are the advantages to a college of having contacts with local businesses? (Why?/Why not?)
- Do you think there are advantages to a company in having contacts with a local college? (Why?/Why not?)
- Do you think the skills people learn in one company are always useful in another company? (Why?/Why not?)

- Thank you. That is the end of the test.

Sample Answer Sheet: Reading

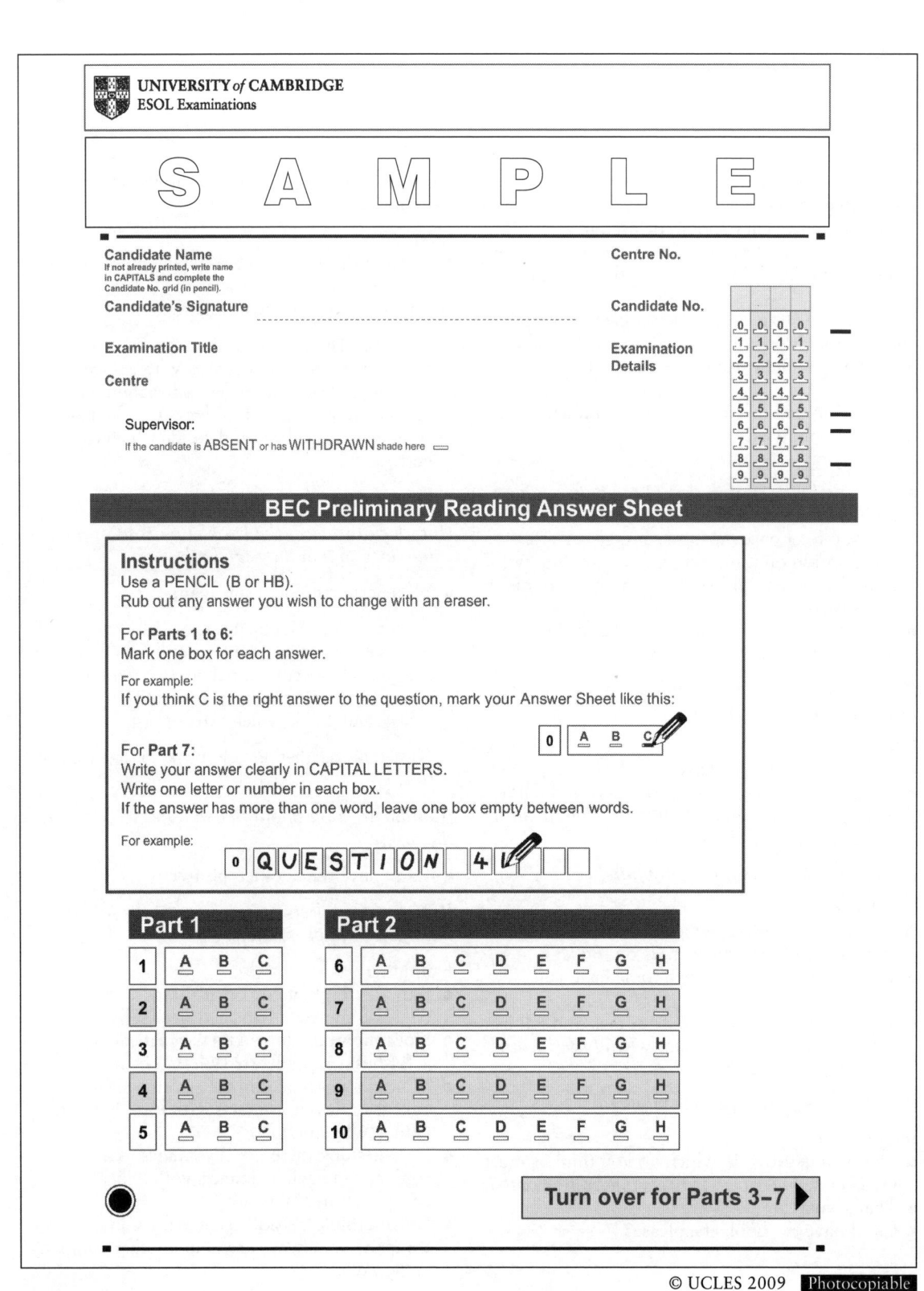

Sample Answer Sheet: Reading

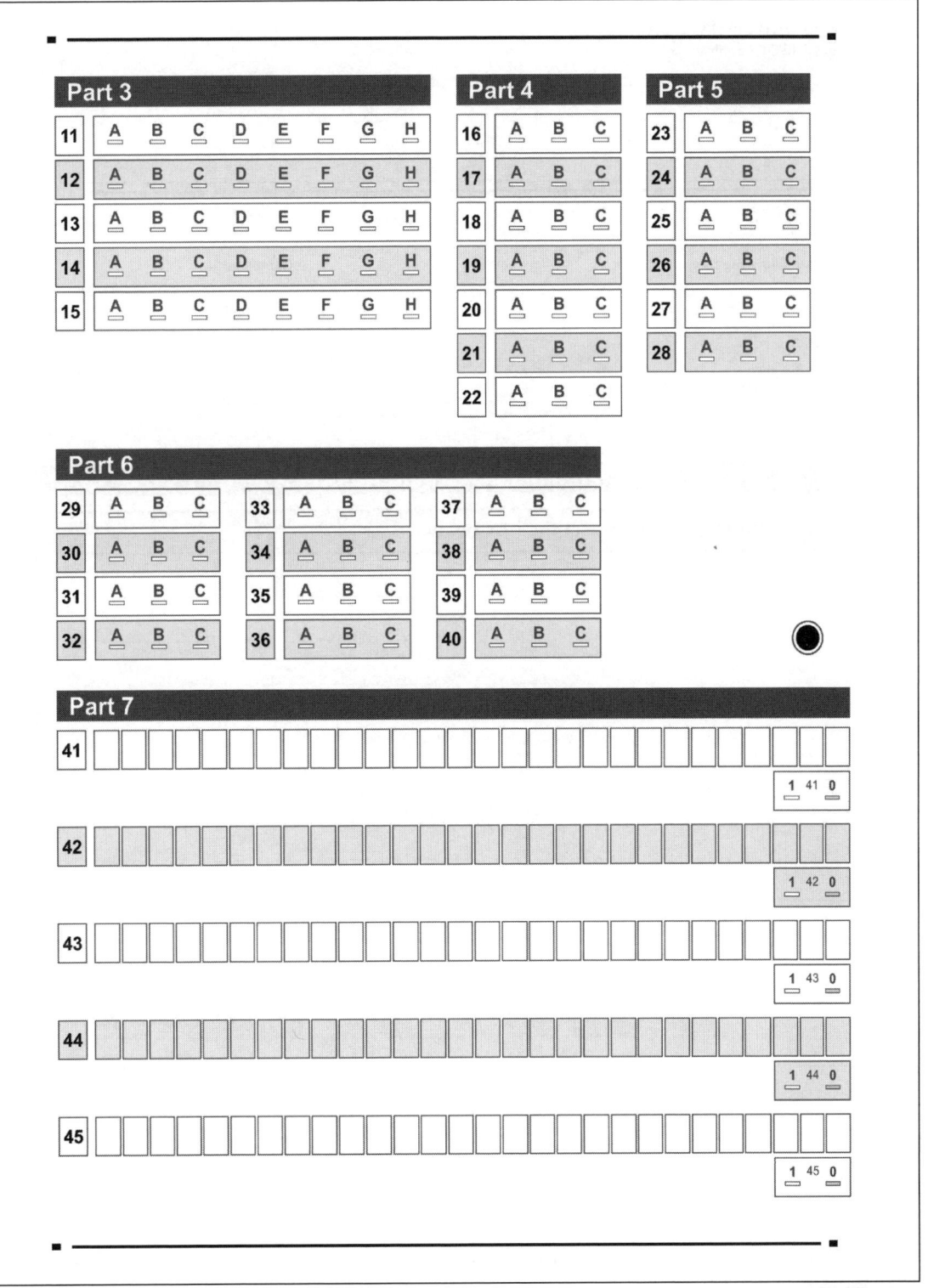

Sample Answer Sheet: Writing

UNIVERSITY of CAMBRIDGE
ESOL Examinations

S A M P L E

Candidate Name
If not already printed, write name in CAPITALS and complete the Candidate No. grid (in pencil).

Candidate's Signature

Examination Title

Centre

Supervisor:
If the candidate is ABSENT or has WITHDRAWN shade here

Centre No.

Candidate No.

Examination Details

BEC Preliminary Writing Answer Sheet

Part 1: Write your answer in the box below.

▶ Write your answer to Part 2 on the other side of this sheet ▶

This section for use by Examiner only

Part 1   0   1   2   3   4   5

© UCLES 2009   Photocopiable

148

Sample Answer Sheet: Writing

Part 2: Write your answer in the box below.

This section for use by Examiner only

| Part 2 | 0 | 1.1 | 1.2 | 2.1 | 2.2 | 3.1 | 3.2 | 4.1 | 4.2 | 5.1 | 5.2 |

Examiner Number

0 1 2 3 4 5 6 7 8 9
0 1 2 3 4 5 6 7 8 9
0 1 2 3 4 5 6 7 8 9
0 1 2 3 4 5 6 7 8 9

Examiner's Signature

© UCLES 2009 Photocopiable

Sample Answer Sheet: Listening

UNIVERSITY of CAMBRIDGE
ESOL Examinations

SAMPLE

Candidate Name
If not already printed, write name in CAPITALS and complete the Candidate No. grid (in pencil).

Candidate's Signature

Examination Title

Centre

Supervisor:
If the candidate is ABSENT or has WITHDRAWN shade here

Centre No.

Candidate No.

Examination Details

BEC Preliminary Listening Answer Sheet

Instructions
Use a PENCIL (B or HB).
Rub out any answer you wish to change with an eraser.

For **Parts 1 and 4**:
Mark one box for each answer.
For example:
If you think C is the right answer to the question, mark your Answer Sheet like this: | 0 | A B C |

For **Parts 2 and 3**:
Write your answer clearly in CAPITAL LETTERS. Write one letter in each box.
If the answer has more than one word, leave one box empty between words.
For example:

| 0 | Y | O | U | R | | A | N | S | W | E | R | | |

Part 1

1. A B C
2. A B C
3. A B C
4. A B C
5. A B C
6. A B C
7. A B C
8. A B C

Part 2

9
10
11
12
13
14
15

Turn over for Parts 3 and 4 ▶

© UCLES 2009 Photocopiable

150

Sample Answer Sheet: Listening

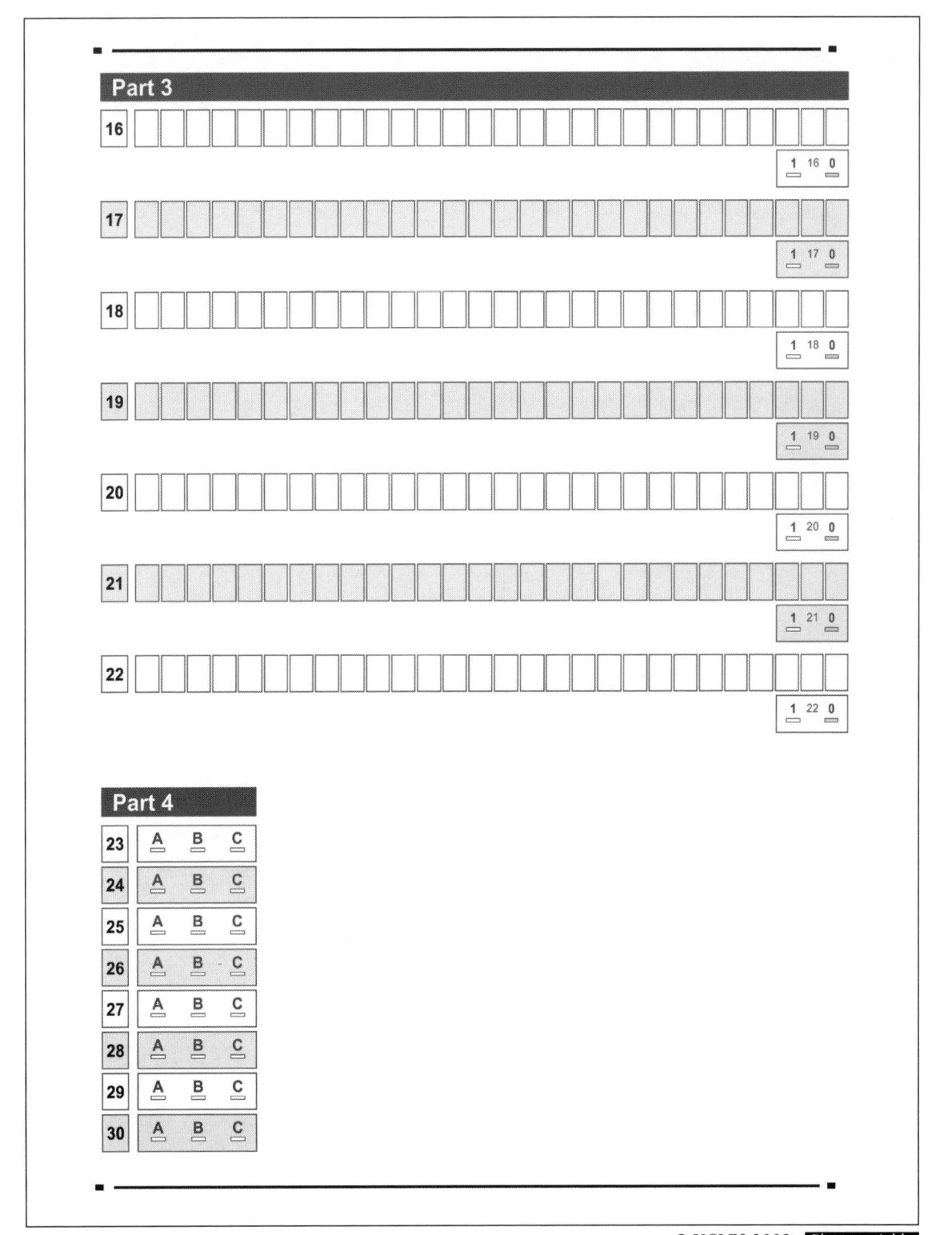

Part 3

16.
17.
18.
19.
20.
21.
22.

Part 4

23. A B C
24. A B C
25. A B C
26. A B C
27. A B C
28. A B C
29. A B C
30. A B C